Interactive Worship
Readings from the
Book of Psalms

A Source Book for Worship Leaders in
Readers Theatre Format

Melvin D. Campbell, Ph.D.

iUniverse LLC
Bloomington

INTERACTIVE WORSHIP READINGS FROM THE BOOK OF PSALMS
A SOURCE BOOK FOR WORSHIP LEADERS IN READERS THEATRE FORMAT

iUniverse books may be ordered through booksellers or by contacting:

iUniverse LLC
1663 Liberty Drive
Bloomington, IN 47403
www.iuniverse.com
1-800-Authors (1-800-288-4677)

ISBN: 978-1-4917-3175-8 (sc)
ISBN: 978-1-4917-3176-5 (e)

Printed in the United States of America.

iUniverse rev. date: 04/29/2014

Contents

Acknowledgements and Thanks

Pastor Dave Peckham
for encouraging me to write

and

Elaine Tarr Dodd
for correcting my many errors

Preface

Stories of the human experiences:
The Psalms in the Christian Bible were written for a variety of reasons. It is nearly impossible to know the historical settings, the purpose of the authors or the intended audiences for which these scriptures were written. From our perspective today the Psalms are words of encouragement, giving us assurance of God's presence in spite of the circumstances in which we find ourselves. As such it is one of the most loved and quoted book in the Christian Bible. It speaks to human existence!

Content of the Psalms
Initially the Psalms were sung with string musical instruments. There has been little effort to duplicate the original music. However there has been some effort to put the thoughts and words to western music. While David receives most of the credit for writing the Psalms, there were certainly other contributors. Their efforts exhibit themselves through some of the following ways:

> nature
> praises
> prayers
> confessions
> God's law
> enemies
> history
> prophecies

Wording of the readings and the King James Version
My approach in the readings is to involve the congregants in an interactive way to experience by the use of words the nature, praises, prayers, confessions, struggles, God's law, enemies, history, prophecies, and parallelism.

The readings are based on the King James Version (KJV) of the Bible for several reasons. The first is that the KJV is in the public domain. While public domain legally refers to be outside of copyright laws, there is a common wide spread use of many of quotes from the KJV in the English language. To eliminate those commonly used phrases would miss the impact of the Psalms.

The second reason for the use of the KJV is the regalness of the language. In an effort to maintain an easy flow of the language, I have changed most of the archaic words to more current and meaningful words for the 21st century Christian and elimination of some words. For example:

art	to	are
thee	to	you
thine	to	your
thou	to	you
thy	to	your

words ending in 'eth' to words ending in 's' as in belongeth becomes belongs

word Selah has been eliminated

I have made no effort to categorize or group the Psalms according to the purpose of the writing. I tried to capture the original meaning of the authors by reproducing the metric rhythm of the text as found in the King James Version of the Bible. The authors of the Psalms were skilled in the use of parallelisms giving their writings a distinctive cadence and appeal. I have tried to keep this in the readings while at the same time modernizing the language. To reproduce the precise intent and purpose of the authors would require knowledge of their culture, musical instruments, and venue for performance. I am privy to only to a small aspect of these!

A Few Words for Worship Leaders

Dynamic Addition to the Worship Service:

Interactive Worship Readings from the Book of Psalms is a companion volume to *Readers Theatre for Christian Worship*[1] and *Interactive Readings for Christian Worship*[2]. The first volume is designed for serious reading of the Psalms involving the choir and the congregants. The second volume is intended to be used by drama groups or church choral reading groups that wish to make presentational readings during the service. The third volume is a series of reading that cast the audience as a character in the Biblical stories.

Readers Theatre is a subset of drama:

These presentational responsive readings are in Readers Theatre format, with two or more Readers at times joined by the Choir and Audience, interpreting the scriptures with their voices. These verbal presentations require no props, costuming, staging, or choreography—just acting with the voice. This makes them attractive for use in worship services, as they focus on the spoken Word of God. The Scriptural scenes unfold in the minds of the Readers, Audience (Congregation) and Choir in praise, doubt, worry, confidence and joy. While David is regarded as the principal author there were undoubtedly others, the authorship takes a background to the emotions expressed in the Psalms.

The responsive readings in this volume have been constructed to recapture at least in part the original feelings, joy, and pathos of the authors. To accomplish this there are at least two readers, who in short 4 to 5 lines give a summary of the reading, then the choir and audience join them in the scriptural reading. Some of the readings are presentational with just the Readers reading.

For the Audience (Congregation) and the Choir to read with expressional emotions called for in the readings, their lines have been restricted to no more than 9 words. This is essential, since the Choir and Audience will be reading the lines for the first time. To set the stage for effective reading by the choir and audience, the readers must have practiced the reading.

Many congregations do not have a choir, so a group of 6 or more can substitute for the choir. Either case the reading must be practiced before it is performed analogous to musical performances in a service.

Reason for structure of the readings:
- The lines to be read are purposely short to enable the readers, congregants, and choir to be able to read expressively.
- Few are skilled readers enough to hold listeners attention. By having two or more readers read one sentence the effect in interpreting the sentence is enhanced.
- More opportunity is given congregants to participate.
- Being read to is not the same as being part of the reading, so the audience and choir are involved in filling the room with the word of God.
- These readings were written to be used either as a call to worship or an introduction to the homily or sermon.

Suggesting for the Readers:
- *Practicing* the reading aloud is essential. Choose Readers of either gender and/or age who are willing to practice and can delivers the lines in expressive voices. No one would think of providing special music without practice. The scripture reading is a performance! Pauses can be very effective in conveying a message, but they must be thought through before the actual reading.
- *Ad-libbing* should not be done, since the readings are tightly scripted. There may be a change in the script by the worship leader, but it must be done before a copy of the reading is given to the Readers, Choir, and Audience.

- *Gesturing* is to be at a minimum and then only if the gesture enhances the reading. It is so easy for Readers to pointlessly move hands, feet, and body about to relieve nervousness, but it only detracts from the spoken word. Don't act but read!
- *Eye contact* with the Audience by the Readers should be kept at a minimum. While most of the Readers' time will be reading from a script, there are times when it is effective to look over the script when part of a line is read to reinforce the words. When so doing the Reader needs to look just over the heads of the Audience and not make eye contact with any one person. The Readers are proclaiming the Word of God!
- *Amplification* is needed for each Reader. However this may not be needed if the venue is small and the Readers have powerful voices.
- *Copies* of the reading need to be provided to the Readers, Choir, and Audience as needed. Many churches now have large screens so the reading is projected. The author's preferred method is to provide all with a paper script.
- *Dress* conservatively! Save party dresses for parties and Hawaiian shirts for Hawaiian luaus. Excess jewelry can easily detract from the reading.

Copyright and uses:

Once this book has been purchased you may use any or all in your worship services. Since it is necessary for the Readers, Congregants, and Choir to have paper copies, all of the readings are made available via email. This will allow downloading all of the scripts so that they can be manipulated to suit your worship format. There is a small charge for the digital copy. Contact me at mdcamp2@gmail.com or 951 688 8564.

Melvin Campbell, Ph.D.
11324 Flower Street
Riverside, California 92505

Melvin D. Campbell, Ph.D.

A Final Few Words:
May the words of our mouths and the thoughts of our minds be acceptable to our Lord.
Good words to you and your congregants.

[1]Campbell, M. and Zackrison, E. (2003) *Readers theatre for Christian worship.* New York: iUniverse.
[2]Campbell, M. and Zackrison, E. (2003) *Interactive readings for Christian worship.* New York: iUniverse.

Blessed Is Mankind
Adapted from Psalm 1
Readers 1,2, Audience, Choir

Introduction

Reader 1: The Scripture today

Reader 2:   deals with men and women

Reader 1:   making choices.

Reader 2: Choices of what they will follow.

Reader 1: Choices that lead to destruction

Reader 2:   or choices that lead to salvation.

Reader 1: This Psalm contrasts the choices
   of the ungodly and the godly

Reader 2:   and their subsequent end.

Reader 1: I invite all to participate

Reader 2:   in the reading of Psalm 1.

Psalm 1

Choir: Blessed is the man

Audience: and blessed is the woman,

Reader 1:   who do not walk where the ungodly walk,

Reader 2:   nor listen to the counsel of the wicked,

Reader 1:   nor stand where sinners stand,

Reader 2:   nor sit where scornful sit.

Choir: The godly delight in the law of the LORD.

Reader 1: They meditate day and night in the counsels
   of the Lord.

Reader 2: And they shall be like a tree planted
   by the rivers of water,

Audience: that brings forth its fruit in season,

Reader 1:   its leaf shall not wither.

Reader 2: Like a tree, whatever the righteous do shall prosper.

Choir:	The ungodly are not so:
Reader 1:	but are like the chaff which the wind drives away.
Reader 2:	The ungodly will not walk where the godly walk.
Audience:	The ungodly will not stand in the judgment.
Reader 1:	Sinners will not remain in the congregation of the righteous.
Audience:	The scornful will scorn no more!
Choir:	For the LORD knows the way of the righteous.
Reader 2:	The way of the ungodly shall perish.

The Son Is Coming

Adapted from Psalm 2

Readers 1,2, Audience, Choir

Introduction

Reader 1: In the Book of Acts, Luke clearly attributes David

Reader 2:   as the author of our reading today.

Reader 1: Questions,

Reader 2:   our Scripture is full of questions

Reader 1:   and unusual answers.

Reader 2: Why do the ungodly operate without God?

Reader 1: In spite of the ungodliness of the ungodly

Reader 2:   we are given the assurance

Reader 1:   that God is still in control through His Son.

Reader 2: Let us read together Psalm 2.

Psalm 2

Choir: Why,

Reader 1:   tell me why the heathen rebel against the Lord and his anointed?

Audience: Why do the heathen rage?

Reader 2: Why do the people make foolish plans?

Reader 1: Why do the kings of nations devise revolt?

Reader 2: Why do the rulers take counsel together against the Lord?

Reader 1: Why do they want to free themselves from the Lord's rules?

Reader 2: Why do they not want to be under God's control?

Reader 1: Whatever their rage, foolish plans, revolts, desire for freedom,

Choir: He still sits in the heavens laughing.

Audience: The LORD shall have them in contempt.

Reader 2: He speaks to them in His wrath,

3

Reader 1:   and afflicts them with mental agitation
in His sore displeasure.

Choir: The LORD said to me,

Reader 1:   Yet have I set my king upon my holy hill of Zion.

Reader 2:   I will declare the decree,

Audience: You are my Son, this day have I begotten you.

Choir: Ask of me,

Reader 1:   and I shall give you the heathen
for your inheritance,

Reader 2:   and the uttermost parts of the earth
for your possession.

Reader 1:   You shall break them with a rod of iron.

Reader 2:   You shall dash them in pieces like a potter's vessel.

Choir: Be wise now therefore, you kings,

Reader 1:   be instructed, you judges of the earth.

Audience: Serve the LORD with fear,

Reader 2:   and rejoice with trembling.

Choir: Adore the Son!

Audience: Blessed are all who put their trust in Him.

Reader 1:   Thanks be to God for these words.

Salvation Belongs to the Lord

Adapted from Psalm 3
Readers 1,2, Audience, Choir

Introduction

Reader 2: David complains to God about his enemies,

Reader 1:   in this case, the enemy is Absalom his son!

Reader 2: He says God has abandoned him.

Reader 1: Then David reaffirms his confidence in God,

Reader 2:   and the continual presence of Him in his life

Reader 1:   in spite of the thousands against him.

Reader 2: Let us read together Psalm 3

Reader 1:   to get a renewed assurance of God's presence,

Reader 2:   a comfort in our lives.

Psalm 3

Reader 1: Lord,

Choir: Why do they prosper who trouble me?

Reader 2: Why are there so many who rise up against me?

Reader 1: Many of them say of my soul,

Reader 2:   there is no help for him in God.

Audience: But you, O Lord, are a shield for me.

Choir: But you, O Lord, are my glory.

Reader 2: O Lord, lift up my head.

Choir: I cried unto the Lord with my voice,

Audience: and he heard!

Reader 1: I lay down and slept,

Reader 2:   while the Lord sustained me.

Audience: When I was awake the Lord still sustained me.

Reader 1: I will not be afraid of ten thousands of people,

Reader 2:   who have set themselves against me.

Audience: O Lord, save me!

Reader 1: O my God, you have smitten all mine enemies

upon the cheek bone.

Reader 2: You have broken the teeth of the ungodly.

Audience: Salvation belongs to you, Lord.

Choir: It is a blessing to be among your people.

Prayer and Answers

Adapted from Psalm 4

Readers 1,2,3, Audience

Introduction

Reader 2: In the first part of our reading the Psalmist

Reader 3:   pleads with the Lord

Reader 2:   to answer his prayers.

Reader 3: Then God responds with

Reader 2:   a series of rhetorical questions

Reader 3:   showing the sinful condition of the Psalmist,

Reader 2:   followed by a call to trust in God.

Reader 3: In the last part of the reading

Reader 2:   the Psalmist thanks the Lord for answered prayer.

Reader 3: Let us now read together Psalm 4.

Psalm 4

Reader 1: O God of my righteousness:

Audience: Hear me when I call.

Reader 1: Give me relief in my distress.

Audience: Have mercy upon me.

Reader 1: Hear my prayer.

Audience: Answer my petitions.

Reader 2: O, you son of man,

Reader 3:   how long will you turn my glory into shame?

Reader 2: How long will you love false gods?

Reader 3: How long will you love delusions?

Reader 2: Know that I the Lord have set apart him who is
  godly for himself.

Reader 3: Stand in awe, and sin not.

Reader 2: Commune with your own heart on your bed,
  and be still.

Reader 3: Offer the sacrifices of righteousness,

Reader 2:   and put your trust in me.

Reader 1:   O, God of my righteousness,

Audience: hear when I call.

Reader 1:   There be many that say,

Audience: Who will show us any good?

Reader 1:   Lord, let the light of your face shine on us.

Audience: You have put gladness in my heart.

Reader 1:   I will both lay me down in peace, and sleep,

Audience: for you, Lord, only makes me dwell in safety.

Reader 1:   Amen.

A Morning Prayer
Adapted from Psalm 5
Readers 1,2, Audience, Choir

Introduction

Reader 1: David prays and pleads

Reader 2:   for God's guidance throughout the day.

Reader 1: He acknowledges how much God hates wickedness.

Reader 2: David is most descriptive of the evils of many

Reader 1:   and ultimately what will become of them.

Reader 2: He then turns his attention to those

Reader 1:   who put their lives in trust to God.

Reader 2: Let us read together David's discourse from Psalm 5.

Psalm 5

Choir: Give ear to my words, O LORD,

Audience: consider my meditation.

Choir: Hearken unto the voice of my cry,

Audience: my King, and my God.

Reader 2: Unto you will I pray.

Reader 1: In the morning my voice you will hear.

Reader 2: In the morning will I direct my prayer unto you.

Reader 1: In the morning I will look up to you,

Reader 2:   for you are not a God who has
no pleasure in wickedness,

Reader 1:   neither shall evil dwell with you.

Choir: The foolish shall not stand in your sight,

Reader 2:   because you hate all workers of iniquity.

Choir: You will destroy them that speak lies.

Reader 1: They are bloody and deceitful men.

Reader 2: But as for me, I will come into your house

Reader 1:   in the midst of your mercy

Reader 2:   and in your fear will I worship.

9

Audience: Lead me, O LORD, in your righteousness

Reader 1:   make your way straight before me.

Choir: There is no faithfulness in the enemies' mouth,

Reader 2:   their inward part are very wicked,

Reader 1:   their throats are open sepulchers,

Reader 2:   their tongues speak lies.

Choir: Destroy them, O God,

Reader 2:   let them fall by their own counsels.

Reader 1:   Cast them out in the multitude
of their transgressions,

Reader 2:   for they have rebelled against you.

Reader 1:   However, those who put their trust in you will have

Audience: their inward parts rejoicing,

Choir: their tongues ever shouting for joy,

Reader 1:   their throats only issuing your praises,

Reader 2:   because you defend them.

Reader 1:   Let those who love your name be joyful in you.

Audience: For you, LORD, will bless the righteous;

Reader 1:   with your favor you will encompass him
as with a shield.

Reader 2:   Thanks be to God for these words.

Plea for Help

Adapted from Psalm 6

Readers 1,2,3, Audience

Introduction

Reader 1:   In the depths of depression David realizes
Reader 2:   his utter helplessness and sinfulness
Reader 1:   in the presence of the Lord.
Reader 2:   He longs for relief from his torturous thoughts
Reader 1:   because of his enemies.
Reader 2:   Finally he finds comfort
Reader 1:   in knowing God will answer his prayers.
Reader 2:   Let us read together Psalm 6,
Reader 1:   knowing we too need the assurance
                of God's forgiveness.

Psalm 6

Reader 3:   O Lord,
Reader 1:   rebuke me not in your anger.
Reader 2:   Discipline me not in your hot displeasure.
Audience: Have mercy upon me, for I am weak.
Reader 3:   Heal me, for my body is in pain
Reader 2:   and my soul is in deep anguish.
Audience: O Lord, how long,
Reader 1:   how long until my soul will be delivered,
Reader 2:   how long until I will be saved for your mercies' sake?
Reader 1:   In death there is no thought of you.
Reader 3:   In the grave who will give you thanks?
Audience: I am weary with my thoughts.
Reader 2:   All night I make my bed to swim with weeping.
Reader 1:   All night I water my couch with my tears.
Reader 3:   My eyes are consumed with grief.
Reader 2:   I fail to see because of my enemies.

Reader 1:   Depart from me, all you who work evil,
Audience: for the Lord has heard my voice.
Reader 3:   The Lord has heard my pleadings.
Audience: The Lord will receive my prayer.
Reader 2:   All my enemies will be ashamed
          and sorely anguished.
Reader 1:   Let them return and be ashamed.
Reader 2:   This ends the reading.

Vengeance Is the Lord's
Adapted from Psalm 7
Readers 1,2, Audience, Choir

Introduction
Reader 1: David apparently has many enemies
Reader 2: who seem to haunt his very existence.
Reader 1: He pleads with the Lord for protection
Reader 2: and to invoke destruction
Reader 1: on his wicked pursuers.
Reader 2: Through all the torment he endures
Reader 1: David ends the reading
Reader 2: praising the Lord!
Reader 1: Read with us David's torturous experience in Psalm 7.

Psalm 7
Reader 1: O LORD my God,
Audience: in you do I put my trust.
Choir: Save me.
Reader 2: from all that persecute me.
Choir: Deliver me,
Reader 1: lest he tear my soul like a lion, rending me in pieces,
Reader 2: while there is none to deliver me.
Audience: O LORD my God,
Reader 1: if there be iniquity in my hands,
Reader 2: if I have rewarded evil unto him that was at peace with me,
Choir: then let the enemy persecute my soul, and take it.
Reader 2: Let him tread down my life upon the earth
Choir: and let him lay my honor in the dust.
Audience: Arise, O LORD,
Reader 1: in your anger,

13

Reader 2: lift up yourself because of the rage of my enemies:

Reader 1: and awake for me to the judgment that you have commanded.

Audience: O LORD, judge the people:

Reader 2: judge me according to my righteousness,

Reader 1: judge me according to my integrity that is in me.

Choir: Let the wickedness of the wicked come to an end.

Audience: Establish the just

Reader 2: for the righteous God tries the hearts and bodies.

Choir: My defense is of God, which saves the upright in heart.

Audience: O Lord, judge the righteous,

Reader 2: be angry at the wicked every day.

Choir: If he turns not from his ways,

Reader 1: the Lord will sharpen his sword,

Reader 2: make ready the bow,

Reader 1: file arrows in his quiver,

Choir: and prepare for him instruments of death.

Reader 1: The wicked have dug a pit of

Choir: iniquity,

Reader 2: mischief,

Choir: falsehood,

Reader 2: violence,

Choir: and have fallen into it!

Reader 1: Their dealings of iniquities,

Reader 2: mischiefs,

Reader 1: falsehoods,

Reader 2: violence,

Reader 1: shall come down upon their own heads.

Audience: But I will praise the LORD according to his righteousness:

Reader 2: and will sing praise to the name of the LORD Most High.

In Praise of Creation
Adapted from Psalm 8
Readers 1,2,3,4

Introduction

Reader 3: The Psalmist extols the Lord of creation

Reader 4:   by citing the entire scope of His creativity.

Reader 3: The unique creation of mankind

Reader 4:   is the crowning work of this loving God.

Reader 3: All else is subject to this crowning work,

Reader 4:   the dominion of mankind.

Reader 3: Allow your mind to dwell on this infinite

Reader 4:   and loving God as Psalm 8 is read.

Psalm 8

Reader 1: O LORD, our Lord,

Reader 3:   how excellent is your name in all the earth!

Reader 4: Who has set your glory above the heavens?

Reader 2: The mouths of children and infants praise you.

Reader 3: You have shown your strength

Reader 4:   and have quieted the enemy and the avenger.

Reader 2: When I consider your heavens,

Reader 1:   the work of your hands,

Reader 4:   the moon and the stars

Reader 3:   which you have put in place,

Reader 2:   what is mankind,

Reader 3:   that you are mindful of him

Reader 4:   and humans that you visit them?

Reader 1: You have made them a little lower than the angels,

Reader 3:   and hast crowned them with glory and honor.

Reader 2: You made them to have dominion over all your creative works.

Reader 4: You have put all things under their feet:

Reader 2:	sheep and oxen,
Reader 1:	beasts of the field,
Reader 3:	fowls of the air,
Reader 4:	fish of the sea,
Reader 2:	and whatever else is in the oceans.
Reader 1:	O LORD, how excellent is your name in all the earth!

What God Does!

Adapted from Psalm 9

Readers 1,2, Audience, Choir

Introduction

Reader 1: The Psalmist begins by praising God

Reader 2:   for his wonderful works.

Reader 1: The writer goes back and forth

Reader 2:   how God should and will deal with the wicked.

Reader 1: Notice how the writer goes back and forth

Reader 2:   how God should and will deal with the righteous.

Reader 1: Then nations will know that they are just human.

Reader 2: We invite all of you to read together how God deals

Reader 1:   with the wicked and righteous in Psalm 9.

Psalm 9

Choir: I will praise you, O Lord,

Reader 1:   with my whole heart

Reader 2:   by showing all your marvelous works,

Reader 1:   being glad and rejoicing in you,

Reader 2:   singing praises to your name,

Choir: O Most High.

Audience: When my enemies are confounded,

Reader 1:   they shall fall and perish at your presence.

Reader 2: You have maintained my right and my cause

Reader 1:   by sitting on the throne judging what is right,

Reader 2:   rebuking the heathen,

Reader 1:   destroying the wicked,

Reader 2:   extinguishing their names forever and ever,

Reader 1:   destroying their cities.

Choir: Thus their memorial is nowhere to be found.

Audience: But the Lord shall endure forever.

Choir: He has prepared His throne for judgment.

Audience:	He shall judge the world in righteousness.
Choir:	He shall minister judgment to the people in uprightness.
Reader 2:	The LORD also will be
Reader 1:	a refuge for the oppressed,
Reader 2:	a refuge in times of trouble,
Reader 1:	a place of safety to those who trust Him.
Reader 2:	LORD, you have not forsaken them that seek you by
Reader 1:	singing praises to the LORD,
Reader 2:	declaring among the people His doings.
Choir:	He forgets not the cry of the humble.
Audience:	Have mercy upon me, O Lord,
Reader 1:	consider my trouble which I suffer of them that hate me.
Reader 2:	You have lifted me up from the gates of death,
Reader 1:	that I may show forth all your praise
Reader 2:	and rejoice in your salvation.
Choir:	The heathen are in the pit that they made:
Reader 1:	in the net which they hid is their own foot taken.
Reader 2:	The Lord is known by the judgment that he executes.
Reader 1:	The wicked are snared in the work of their own hands.
Reader 2:	They shall be turned into hell,
Reader 1:	because they forgot that the Lord is God.
Choir:	The needy shall not always be forgotten:
Reader 2:	the expectation of the poor will not perish forever.
Audience:	Arise,
Reader 1:	let no man prevail,
Reader 2:	let the heathen be judged in your sight.
Audience:	Put them in fear, O LORD,
Reader 1:	that the nations may know they are but men.
Reader 2:	This ends the reading.

Wicked and the Poor
Adapted from Psalm 10
Readers 1,2,3,4

Introduction

Reader 2: This reading, through a series of questions

Reader 3:   and statements indicts the person

Reader 2:   who has no regard for the less fortunate and poor.

Reader 3: Finally there is an appeal to God

Reader 2:   to crush the behavior.

Reader 3: Listen as we read from Psalm 10.

Psalm 10

Reader 1: Why, O Lord, why?

Reader 3: Why do you hide yourself from the poor?

Reader 2: Why do the wicked persecute the poor?

Reader 3: Why do the wicked boast of their heart's desire?

Reader 2: Why do the wicked bless the covetous,
    whom the Lord hates?

Reader 1: Why do the wicked not seek after God?

Reader 4: God is not in their thoughts.

Reader 3: Why do the wicked always flourish?

Reader 2: The judgments of God are ignored.

Reader 4: I just laugh at my enemies.

Reader 3: In his arrogance he says,

Reader 4:   No one can injure me.

Reader 2: The wicked is full . . .

Reader 1:   of curses,

Reader 3:   of lies,

Reader 2:   of fraud

Reader 3:   of mischief,

Reader 2:   of self-love.

Reader 1: He sits in the lurking places of the villages.

Reader 3:   In the secret places he murders the innocent.

Reader 2:   He watches the poor secretly as a hunter in a blind.

Reader 4:   He does catch the poor,

Reader 1:   drawing them into his evil net.

Reader 3:   He says in his heart,

Reader 4:   God will never see it.

Reader 1:   Arise, O Lord, lift up your hand,

Reader 3:   forget not the humble.

Reader 1:   Why do the wicked men taunt God?

Reader 2:   Why do they say in their hearts,

Reader 4:   God will never see it?

Reader 3:   But you, God, have seen,

Reader 2:   the poor,

Reader 3:   the fatherless.

Reader 4:   These are my victims!

Reader 1:   God, you are the helper of the helpless.

Reader 3:   You are the father of the fatherless.

Reader 2:   Break the arm of the wicked and the evil man.

Reader 4:   The Lord is King forever and ever.

Reader 1:   The heathen are perished out of His land.

Reader 3:   Lord, you have heard the desire
      of the humble and poor.

Reader 2:   Prepare their hearts,

Reader 1:   so they listen to your voice.

Reader 3:   Judge the fatherless and the oppressed,

Reader 4:   that the men of the earth may oppress no more.

Trusting the Lord
Adapted from Psalm 11
Readers 1,2, Audience

Introduction

Reader 1:   The Psalmist affirms his trust in the Lord

Reader 2:   as the only safe place to be.

Reader 1:   He also verifies that the Lord

Reader 2:   will see to the final end of sinners.

Reader 1:   Let us now read together Psalm 11.

Psalm 11

Reader 2:   In the Lord I put my trust!

Audience: Why would I want to

Reader 1:   to flee as a bird to your mountain?

Reader 2:   The wicked bend their bow,

Reader 1:   they make ready their arrow upon the string,

Reader 2:   that they may shoot at the upright in heart.

Reader 1:   If the foundations be destroyed,

Reader 2:   what can the righteous do?

Audience: The Lord is in His holy temple.

Reader 1:   The Lord's throne is in heaven:

Reader 2:   His eyes see and observe the children of men.

Audience: The Lord examines the righteous,

Reader 2:   but the wicked and those who love violence
His soul hates.

Reader 1:   On the wicked He shall rain snares,

Reader 2:   fire and brimstone,

Reader 1:   and a horrible tempest.

Reader 2:   This shall be the portion of their cup.

Audience: The Lord is righteous,

Reader 2:   and righteous people will see His face.

The Fool
Adapted from Psalm 14
Readers 1,2

Introduction

Reader 1: David gives a description of the godless,

Reader 2:   whom he calls fools!

Reader 1: He longs for the day

Reader 2:   when captivity is no more.

Reader 1: Listen as we read from Psalm 14.

Psalm 14

Reader 2: Fools say in their hearts, there is no God.

Reader 1: Fools are corrupt, they have done vile works,

Reader 2:   there are none that do good.

Reader 1: The LORD looked down from heaven upon the children of men,

Reader 2:   to see if there were any who did understand and seek Him.

Reader 1: They are all gone aside.

Reader 2: They are all together become corrupt.

Reader 1: There are none that do good, no, not one.

Reader 2: They are fools!

Reader 1: Have all the workers of iniquity no knowledge?

Reader 2: They eat up my people as they eat bread,

Reader 1:   and call not upon the LORD.

Reader 2: They were in great fear,

Reader 1:   for God is in the generation of the righteous.

Reader 2: Fools have dishonored the affairs of the poor,

Reader 1:   but the LORD is their refuge.

Reader 2: Oh, that the salvation of Israel would come out of Zion!

Reader 1:   When the LORD brings back
               the captivity of his people,
Reader 2:   Jacob shall rejoice,
Reader 1:   and Israel shall be glad.
Reader 2:   This ends the reading.

Characteristics of the Righteous
Adapted from Psalm 15
Readers 1,2, Audience

Introduction
Reader 1: This Psalm of David

Reader 2:   outlines the attributes

Reader 1:   of one who expects to dwell with God.

Reader 2: Join us in reading Psalm 15.

Psalm 15
Reader 1: Lord, who shall abide in your tabernacle?

Audience: He who walks blameless,

Reader 2:   and does what is righteous,

Reader 1:   and speaks the truth from his heart.

Reader 2: Who shall dwell in your holy hill?

Audience: He who does not gossip about his neighbor,

Reader 1:   nor does no wrong to his neighbor,

Reader 2:   nor shames his neighbor in any way.

Reader 1: He despises a vile person,

Reader 2:   but he honors them that fear the Lord.

Reader 1: This is the oath of the Lord

Reader 2:   and He will not change!

Reader 1: Lord, who shall abide in your tabernacle?

Reader 2: He who lends his money without usury,

Audience: nor takes bribes against the innocent.

Reader 1: He that does these things shall never be moved.

Audience: He shall abide and dwell with the Lord.

Reader 2: This ends the reading.

God Is the Destination
Adapted from Psalm 16
Readers 1,2, Audience

Introduction

Reader 1:   David recognizes his nothingness before God,

Reader 2:   yet he praises Him for His advice.

Reader 1:   David understands that the path that
God has set before him,

Reader 2:   leads only to joy.

Reader 1:   Let us read together Psalm 16.

Psalm 16

Reader 2:   Preserve me, O God,

Reader 1:   for in you do I put my trust.

Reader 2:   I said to the Lord,

Audience: you are my Lord.

Reader 2:   Apart from you I am nothing.

Reader 1:   But to the saints that are in the earth,

Reader 2:   in whom is all my delight.

Reader 1:   Even so, sorrows will be multiplied

Reader 2:   who hasten after another god.

Reader 1:   Their drink offerings of blood I will not accept,

Reader 2:   nor take up their names on my lips.

Audience: The LORD is the portion

Reader 1:   of my inheritance and of my cup.

Audience: He maintains my life.

Reader 1:   I have a good heritage.

Audience: I will bless the Lord, who has given me counsel.

Reader 2:   My heart also instructs me at night.

Reader 1:   I have set the LORD always before me,

Reader 2:   because he is at my right hand,

Audience: I shall not be moved.

Reader 2:   Therefore my heart is glad,

Reader 1:   and my entire body rests in your hope.

Reader 2:   You will not leave me in the grave,

Reader 1:   rather you will show me the path of life.

Audience: In your presence is fullness of joy.

Reader 1:   At your right hand there are pleasures for evermore.

David's Prayer
Adapted from Psalm 18
Readers 1,2, Audience

Introduction

Reader 1: David's prayer in Psalm 18

Reader 2: comes from his trying experience with his foes

Reader 1: and with a deep understanding

Reader 2: of the power and guiding presence of the Lord God.

Reader 1: In many aspects this prayer could also be ours.

Reader 2: Let us now read and pray with David, Psalm 18.

Psalm 18

Reader 1: I will love you, O LORD, my strength.

Audience: The LORD is my rock,

Reader 2: my fortress,

Reader 1: my deliverer,

Reader 2: my God,

Reader 1: in whom I will trust.

Audience: He is my shield,

Reader 1: the horn of my salvation,

Reader 2: and my high tower.

Audience: I will call upon the LORD,

Reader 1: who is worthy to be praised

Reader 2: so shall I be saved from my enemies.

Reader 1: The sorrows of death surround me,

Reader 2: and the floods of ungodly men made me afraid.

Reader 1: In my distress I called upon the LORD.

Audience: He heard my voice.

Reader 2: He delivered me from my strong enemies,

Reader 1: and from those who hate me,

Reader 2: for they were too strong for me.

Audience: He delivered me,

Reader 2:   because he delighted in me.
Reader 1: The LORD rewarded me according to my righteousness.
Reader 2: With the merciful you will show yourself merciful.
Reader 2: With the upright you will show yourself upright.
Reader 1: For you, O Lord, will save the afflicted people.
Reader 2: For you, O Lord, will light my candle.
Audience: You will turn my darkness into light.
Reader 1: As for God, his way is perfect.
Reader 2: He is a shield to all those who trust in Him.
Audience: For who is God, save the LORD?
Reader 1: Or who is a rock, save our God?
Reader 2: It is God that gives me strength,
Reader 1:   and makes my way perfect.
Reader 2: Lord, you have given me the shield of your salvation.
Reader 1: I have pursued my enemies, and overtaken them,
Reader 2:   neither did I turn again till they were consumed.
Audience: The Lord lives, and blessed be the rock.
Reader 1: Let the God of my salvation be exalted.
Reader 2: It is God that avenged me,
Reader 1:   and subdued the people under me
Reader 1:   and sing praises unto your name.
Audience: The Lord lives, and blessed be the rock.
Reader 2: Great deliverance He given to his king
Reader 1:   and shows mercy to his anointed, to David,
Reader 2:   and to his seed for evermore.
Audience: Therefore will I give thanks to you, O Lord,
Reader 1: Amen.

The Heavens Declare . . .

Adapted from Psalm 19
Readers 1,2, Audience, Choir

Introduction

Reader 1: Psalm 19 is one of the most poetic

Reader 2:   and well known Psalms.

Reader 1: God's glory is shown to transcend this earth,

Reader 2:   encompassing the universe.

Reader 1: The Psalmist enumerates what is His glory,

Reader 2:   His law, His commandments, His actions.

Reader 1: Then finally the author realizes his own errors

Reader 2:   and prays that his thoughts
            and life be acceptable to God.

Reader 1: Let us join together in reading Psalm 19.

Psalm 19

Choir: The heavens declare the glory of God

Audience: and the firmament shows His handiwork.

Reader 1: Day after day they speak,

Reader 2:   and night after night show language.

Reader 1: There is no speech nor language,

Reader 2:   where their voice is not heard.

Reader 1: Their silent voice is gone out through all the earth,

Reader 2:   and their words to the end of the world.

Choir: In them He has set a place for the sun,

Reader 1:   which is as a bridegroom coming out of his
            chamber,

Audience: and as a strong man to run a race.

Reader 1: His going forth is from the end of the heavens,

Reader 2:   and His circuit to the ends of the universe.

Audience: The law of the LORD is perfect,

Choir: converting the soul.

29

Audience::	The testimony of the LORD is sure,
Choir:	making wise the simple.
Audience::	The statutes of the LORD are right,
Choir:	rejoicing the heart.
Audience::	The commandments of the LORD are pure,
Choir:	enlightening the soul.
Audience::	The fear of the LORD is pure,
Choir:	enduring forever.
Reader 1:	The judgments of the LORD are true
	and righteous altogether.
Choir:	More to be desired are they than gold,
Audience:	yea than much fine gold,
Choir:	sweeter also than honey and the honeycomb.
Reader 2:	Moreover by them is your servant warned
Reader 1:	and in keeping of them there is great reward.
Audience:	Who can understand his own errors?
Choir:	Forgive my hidden sins
Reader 2:	and presumptuous sins.
Reader 1:	Let them not have dominion over me,
Reader 2:	then shall I be upright
Reader 1:	and be innocent from the great transgression.
Choir:	Let the words of my mouth,
Audience:	and the meditation of my heart,
Choir:	be acceptable in your sight,
Readers 1:	O LORD, my strength, and my redeemer.
Reader 2:	Amen.

Answered Prayer
Adapted from Psalm 20
Readers 1,2, Audience

Introduction

Reader 1: This Psalm is one of encouragement and confidence
Reader 2:   in the strength and saving power of God,
Reader 1:   thus giving cause for rejoicing.
Reader 2: Now let us read together Psalm 20.

Psalm 20

Reader 1: The LORD will hear you in the day of trouble.
Reader 2: The name of the God of Jacob will defend you.
Reader 1: He will help you from the sanctuary,
Reader 2:   and strengthen you out of Zion.
Audience: He will remember all your offerings,
Reader 2:   and accept your burnt sacrifice.
Reader 1: He will grant you according to your desires,
Reader 2:   and fulfill all your pleas.
Audience: Rejoice in salvation.
Reader 1: Lift up the banner of salvation.
Reader 2: The LORD has granted all your petitions.
Audience: Now know I that the LORD saves.
Reader 1: He hears from his holy heaven with the saving strength
    of his right hand.
Reader 2: Some trust in chariots,
Reader 1:   some in horses,
Audience: but, we trust in the name of the LORD.
Reader 2: Many are brought down and fallen,
Reader 1:   but we are risen, and stand upright.
Audience: Save us Lord.
Reader 1: Let our king hear us when we call.
Reader 2: Thanks be to God for these words.

David's Thanksgiving
Adapted from Psalm 21
Readers 1,2,3,4

Introduction
Reader 1:   This Psalm is one of thanksgiving.
Reader 2:   David, the king, celebrates
Reader 1:   his victory over his enemies.
Reader 2:   Finally note the ultimate end
            of the enemies of David and God.
Reader 1:   Now enter into David's experience
            as we read Psalm 21.

Psalm 21
Reader 3:   O Lord, the king finds joy in your strength
Reader 4:   and in your salvation he greatly rejoices!
Reader 3:   You have given him his heart's desire,
Reader 4:   and have not withheld the request of his lips.
Reader 3:   O Lord, you provided him
            with the blessings of goodness.
Reader 4:   You have set a crown of pure gold on his head.
Reader 1:   The king asked for life,
Reader 2:   you gave it to him, even length of days
            forever and ever.
Reader 3:   His glory is great in your salvation,
Reader 4:   honor and majesty have you laid on him.
Reader 2:   You have made him the most blessed forever.
Reader 1:   You have made him exceeding glad
            with your presence.
Reader 3:   For the king trusts in the LORD,
Reader 4:   and through the mercy of the Most High
            he shall not be moved.
Reader 3:   Your hand shall find all mine enemies,

Reader 1:   your right hand shall find those that hate you.

Reader 2:   You will make them as a fiery oven
              in the time of your anger.

Reader 4:   The LORD shall swallow them in His wrath,

Reader 1:   and the fire shall consume them.

Reader 2:   Their fruit you will destroy from the earth

Reader 3:   and their seed from among the children of men,

Reader 4:   because they intended evil against you.

Reader 3:   They imagined a mischievous device,

Reader 4:   which they are not able to perform.

Reader 3:   O Lord, be exalted, in your own strength:

Reader 4:   so will we sing and praise your power.

Reader 1:   This ends the reading.

The Lord Is my Shepherd
Adapted from Psalm 23
Reader, Audience, Choir

Introduction

Reader: Without question Psalm 23 is the most widely known and read of all the Psalms! While it is based in a pastoral setting it has transcended the centuries to still give meaning to the modern world. It is probably the most memorized scripture in the entire Bible. Let's read it anew with a deep conviction of its importance in our lives.

Psalm 23

Reader: The LORD is my shepherd

Audience: I shall not want.

Reader: He makes me lie down in green pastures.

Choir: He leads me beside still waters.

Audience: He restores my soul.

Reader: He leads me in the paths of righteousness

Choir: for His name's sake.

Reader: Yea, though I walk through the valley of the shadow of death,

Audience: I will fear no evil,

Reader: for you are with me.

Audience: Your rod and staff comfort me.

Reader: You prepare a table before me

Choir: in the presence of my enemies.

Reader: You anoint my head with oil,

Audience: my cup runs over.

Choir: Surely goodness and mercy

Audience: shall follow me all the days of my life

Reader: and I will dwell in the house of the LORD forever.

Audience: The Lord is my shepherd.

King of Glory
Adapted from Psalm 24
Reader 1,2, Audience, Choir

Introduction
Reader 1: In our reading the Psalmist acknowledges
the dominion and ownership of the Lord of hosts
Reader 2: and the traits of those who will live with Him.
Reader 1: Lastly, an account is given of the triumphal entry
Reader 2: of the Lord into our lives.
Reader 1: Let us now read together
Reader 2: about the King of Glory from Psalm 24.

Psalm 24
Reader 1: Who is this King of glory?
Audience: The LORD of hosts,
Choir: He is the King of glory.
Reader 2: The earth is the LORD's,
Reader 1: and everything in it
Reader 2: and they that dwell therein.
Reader 1: He founded it upon the seas,
Reader 2: and established it upon the floods.
Reader 1: Who shall ascend to the mountain of the LORD?
Reader 2: Who shall stand in His holy place?
Audience: A generation of people who seek Him.
Reader 2: People . . .
Audience: who have clean hands,
Choir: who have pure hearts,
Audience: who do not have self-love,
Choir: who do not swear falsely.
Reader 1: Those shall receive the blessing from the LORD
Reader 2: and righteousness from the God of his salvation.
Reader 1: Soooooo . . .

Reader 2:   Lift up your heads, O ye gates,

Reader 1:   and be ye lifted up, ye everlasting doors,

Audience: and the King of glory shall come in,

Choir: and the King of glory shall come in.

Reader 1:   Who is this King of glory?

Audience: The LORD strong and mighty,

Choir: the LORD mighty in battle.

Reader 1:   Lift up your heads, O ye gates:

Reader 2:   even lift them up, ye everlasting doors,

Audience: and the King of glory shall come in.

Reader 1:   Who is this King of glory?

Audience: The LORD of hosts,

Choir: He is the King of glory.

Reader 2:   The earth is the LORD's,

Reader 1:   and everything in it.

The Lord Is my Light
Adapted from Psalm 27
Readers 1,2, Audience, Choir

Introduction

Reader 1: David's Psalm is one of confidence

Reader 2:   in the guidance and protection of the Lord,

Reader 1:   even though surrounded by people

Reader 2:   who would like to destroy him.

Reader 1: This prayer ends with advice to all of us:

Reader 2: Wait on the Lord.

Reader 1: Let us join together in reading Psalm 27.

Psalm 27

Choir: The Lord is my light and my salvation,

Audience: whom shall I fear?

Reader 1: Though an army should encamp against me,

Reader 2:   my heart shall not fear.

Reader 1: Though war should rise against me,

Reader 2:   in this will I be confident,

Choir: the Lord is the strength of my life.

Audience: O whom shall I be afraid?

Reader 1: Though my enemies and my foes,

Reader 2:   came upon me to devour me;

Reader 1:   they stumbled and fell.

Choir: One thing have I desired of the Lord,

Audience: that I may dwell in His house

Reader 1:   all the days of my life,

Reader 2:   to behold the beauty of the Lord.

Reader 1: In the time of trouble He shall hide me in His pavilion.

Reader 2: In the secret of His tabernacle shall He hide me.

Reader 1: He shall set me up upon a rock,

Reader 2:   therefore, I will sing praises to the Lord.

Choir:	Hear, O Lord, when I cry with my voice
Audience:	have mercy upon me by answering me.
Reader 1:	The Lord said, seek my face.
Reader 2:	My heart said;
Audience:	Your face, Lord, will I seek.
Reader 1:	So Lord, do not hide your face from me.
Reader 2:	Do not put your servant away in anger.
Reader 1:	Do not leave me.
Reader 2:	Do not forsake me,
Reader 1:	O God of my salvation.
Choir:	You have been my help.
Reader 1:	Though my father and my mother forsake me,
Reader 2:	the Lord will receive me.
Reader 1:	Teach me your way, O Lord, lead me in a plain path.
Reader 2:	Deliver me from my enemies
Reader 1:	for false witnesses are risen up against me.
Reader 2:	I am positive that I will see the goodness of the LORD in the land of the living.
Choir:	Wait on the Lord.
Audience:	Be of good courage,
Reader 1:	and He shall strengthen your heart.
Reader 2:	Wait, I say, on the Lord.
Reader 1:	Thanks be to God for these words.

God Our Help and Strength
Adapted from Psalm 33
Reader 1,2, Audience, Choir

Introduction

Reader 2: Our reading gives praise and adoration to the Lord.

Reader 1: The Psalmist acknowledges the creative power of God.

Reader 2: Nothing will stand in the way

Reader 1:   of the Lord accomplishing His purposes.

Reader 2: While the Lord works out His plans, we wait in hope.

Reader 1: Let's read together Psalm 33.

Psalm 33

Reader 1: Rejoice in the LORD, you righteous,

Reader 2:   for praise is fitting for the upright.

Choir: Praise the LORD with harp.

Reader 1: Sing to Him with the psaltery.

Choir: Sing to Him a new song.

Audience: For the word of the LORD is right

Reader 2:   and all His works are done in truth.

Reader 1: He loves righteousness and judgment.

Reader 2: The earth is full of His goodness.

Reader 1: By the word of the LORD the heavens were made

Reader 2:   and all the stars by the breath of His mouth.

Reader 1: He gathered the waters of the sea together as a heap.

Audience: Let all the earth fear the LORD!

Reader 2: Let all the inhabitants of the world

Reader 1:   stand in awe of Him.

Choir: For He spoke, and it was done.

Audience: He commanded and it stood fast.

Reader 2: The LORD brings the counsel of the heathen to nothing.

Reader 1: He makes the devices of the people of none effect.

Audience:	The counsels of the LORD stand forever,
Reader 1:	the thoughts of His heart to all generations.
Reader 2:	Blessed is the nation whose god is the LORD.
Reader 1:	Blessed are the people whom
	He hath chosen for His own inheritance.
Choir:	The LORD looks from heaven,
Reader 2:	He sees all the inhabitants of the earth.
Reader 1:	He considers all their works.
Reader 2:	No king is saved by his army
Reader 1:	nor is a mighty man delivered by his strength.
Reader 2:	A horse is a vain hope for safety,
Reader 1:	neither shall any be delivered by its great strength.
Choir:	Behold, the eye of the LORD is . . .
Reader 2:	is on them that fear Him,
Reader 1:	is on them that hope in His mercy
Reader 2:	to deliver their soul from death
Reader 1:	and to keep them alive in famine.
Audience:	We wait for the LORD
Choir:	for He is our help and our shield.
Reader 2:	Our hearts will rejoice in Him,
Reader 1:	because we have trusted in His holy name.
Reader 2:	Let your mercy, O LORD,
Reader 1:	be on us as we hope in you.
Reader 2:	Thanks be to God for these words.

David's Testimony
Adapted from Psalm 34
Reader 1,2,3,4, Choir

Introduction

Reader 1: In our reading David recounts the many blessings

Reader 2:   he has received from the Lord.

Reader 1: He gives an invitation to others

Reader 2:   to experience what he has experienced

Reader 1:   and what lifestyle they need to have.

Reader 2: This Psalm leaves no doubt

Reader 1:   that David is a man after God's own heart!

Reader 2: Now the reading from Psalm 34.

Psalm 34

Reader 1: I will bless the LORD at all times:

Reader 2:   His praise shall continually be on my lips.

Reader 4: My inmost thoughts glory in the LORD;

Reader 3:   those less fortunate hear and rejoice.

Choir: O magnify the LORD with me.

Reader 1: Let us exalt His name together.

Reader 3: I sought the LORD, and He heard and answered me.

Choir: He delivered us from all our fears.

Reader 4: They looked to Him and were not ashamed.

Reader 3: This poor man cried,

Reader 2:   and the LORD heard him,

Reader 1:   and saved him out of all his troubles.

Reader 2: The angel of the LORD camps around them

Reader 4:   who fear Him and delivers them.

Choir: Taste and see that the LORD is good.

Reader 1: Blessed is the man that trusts in Him.

Choir: Fear the LORD, you saints,

Reader 3:   for those who fear Him lack nothing.

Reader 2: The young lions do lack and suffer hunger,

Reader 1:   but they that seek the Lord lack no good thing.

Reader 4: Listen my children,

Reader 3:   I will teach you the fear of the Lord.

Choir: If you desire life, and love many days, then:

Reader 3:   Keep your tongue from evil.

Reader 2:   Stop speaking guile with your lips.

Reader 3:   Depart from evil.

Reader 4:   Do good.

Reader 1:   Seek peace and pursue it.

Choir: The eyes of the Lord are on the righteous,

Reader 2: His ears are open to their cry.

Reader 4: However, the face of the Lord
    is against them that do evil,

Reader 3:   to cut off the remembrance of them
    from the earth.

Choir: The righteous cry, and the Lord hears

Reader 4:   and delivers them out of their troubles.

Reader 1: He heals a broken heart and a contrite spirit

Reader 2:   delivering them out of afflictions.

Reader 1: He keeps all the bones;

Reader 2:   not one of them is broken.

Choir: Evil shall slay the wicked

Reader 4:   and they that hate the righteous come to no good.

Reader 1: The Lord redeems His servants;

Choir: and no one who trusts in the Lord shall be
    condemned.

Reader 2: This ends the reading.

He Sustains

Adapted from Psalm 37
Reader 1,2, Audience, Choir

Introduction

Reader 1: We will be reading the last part of Psalm 37.

Reader 2: David explains the care of a loving God

Reader 1: who sustains us when we fall

Reader 2: and the results of trusting God.

Reader 1: Let us read together Psalm 37

Psalm 37

Reader 1: When the steps of a good man are ordered
by the LORD,

Audience: He is delighted.

Reader 2: Though persons may fall,

Reader 1: they will not be utterly cast down,

Audience: for the LORD holds them in His hand.

Reader 1: I have been young,

Reader 2: and now am old:

Reader 1: yet have I not seen the righteous forsaken,

Reader 2: nor His children begging for bread.

Reader 1: He is ever merciful, and gives freely,

Reader 2: and His children are blessed.

Choir: Depart from evil, do good

Audience: and live for evermore.

Reader 1: For the LORD loves judgment
and forsakes not His saints.

Reader 2: They are preserved for ever,

Reader 1: but the children of the wicked shall be destroyed.

Audience: The righteous will inherit the land,

Choir: and dwell therein for ever.

Reader 2: The mouth of the righteous speaks wisdom,

Reader 1:   and his tongue talks of judgment.

Reader 2:   The law of his God is in his heart,

Reader 1:   none of his steps goes astray.

Reader 2:   The wicked watch the righteous,
       and desire to slay them.

Reader 1:   The LORD will not leave them in their hand,

Reader 2:   nor condemn them when he is judged.

Choir: Wait on the LORD,

Audience: and keep His way

Choir: and you will inherit the earth.

Reader 1:   When the wicked are cut off, you will see it.

Reader 2:   I have seen the wicked in great power

Reader 1:   and spreading themselves like a green bay tree.

Reader 2:   Yet they passed away, and, lo, they were not.

Reader 1:   I sought them, but they could not be found.

Audience: Mark the perfect man.

Choir: Consider the upright

Reader 1:   for the end of that person is peace.

Reader 2:   But the transgressors shall be destroyed together.

Reader 1:   The ultimate end of the wicked will be destruction.

Audience: But the salvation of the righteous is of the LORD.

Choir: He is their strength in the time of trouble.

Reader 1:   The LORD shall help them and deliver them.

Reader 2:   He shall deliver them from the wicked
       and save them,

Reader 1:   because they trust in Him.

Reader 2:   Thanks be to God for these words.

He Heard My Cry

Adapted from Psalm 40

Reader 1,2, Audience

Introduction

Reader 1: Psalm 40 is a testimony of God's goodness

Reader 2:   and the personal benefits of trusting Him.

Reader 1: The writer lists the good things He has done

Reader 2:   in the great congregation,

Reader 1:   yet he fears destruction from evil ones.

Reader 2: The Psalm ends with the words,

Reader 1:   Lord, think of me.

Reader 2: Let us read together Psalm 40.

Psalm 40

Reader 1: I waited patiently for the LORD.

Audience: He heard my cry.

Reader 2: He brought me up out of a horrible pit,

Reader 1:   out of the miry clay,

Reader 2:   set my feet upon a rock,

Audience: established my goings,

Reader 1:   put a new song on my lips.

Audience: Praises to our God!

Reader 1: Happy are those who

Reader 2:   see,

Reader 1:   fear,

Audience: and make the LORD their trust,

Reader 2:   and don't respect the proud nor liars.

Reader 1: Many, O LORD, are your wonderful works.

Audience: They are more than can be numbered.

Reader 2: Oh Lord, you do not desire

Reader 1:   sacrifice and offerings or burnt offering.

Audience: Rather I delight to do your will.

Reader 1:   Your law is in my heart.

Reader 2:   In the great congregation

Audience: I have preached righteousness.

Reader 1:   I have not hidden your righteousness.

Reader 2:   I have declared your faithfulness
                        and your salvation.

Audience: I have not concealed your loving kindness.

Reader 1:   Withhold not your tender mercies from me,

Reader 2:   let your loving kindness

Reader 1:   and your truth continually preserve me.

Audience: Yet many evils surround me.

Reader 2:   My iniquities have taken hold upon me,

Reader 1:   so that I am not able to look up.

Reader 2:   They are more than the hairs of my head.

Audience: Be pleased, O LORD, to deliver me.

Reader 1:   O LORD, make haste to help me

Reader 2:   from those who seek to destroy my soul

Reader 1:   or wish me to do evil.

Reader 2:   Let all those who seek you rejoice and be glad.

Reader 1:   Let all who love your salvation say continually,

Audience: The LORD be magnified.

Reader 2:   Even though I am poor and needy,

Reader 1:   Lord, think of me.

Reader 2:   O my God, you are my help and my deliverer.

Reader 1:   Amen.

Sons of Korah
Adapted from Psalm 42
Reader 1,2, Audience, Choir

Introduction

Reader 1:   This reading goes from desiring
            a relationship with God
Reader 2:   to one of depression,
Reader 1:   thinking that God is not there.
Reader 2:   The reading ends with the author
Reader 1:   praising God for his life.
Reader 2:   Let us read together from Psalm 42.

Psalm 42

Reader 1:   As the deer pants after the water brooks,
Reader 2:   so pants my soul after you, O God.
Audience: My soul thirsts for God.
Choir: Our souls thirsts for the living God.
Reader 1:   When can I come and appear before God?
Reader 2:   My tears have been continually with me day and
            night.
Reader 1:   People always say unto me,
Reader 2:   Where is your God?
Reader 1:   When I remember these things
Reader 2:   I pour out my soul
Reader 1:   for I had gone with the crowd,
Reader 2:   going with them to the house of God,
Reader 1:   with the voice of joy and praise.
Reader 2:   Why am I cast down?
Reader 1:   Why am I so distressed?
Audience: Place your hope in God.
Choir: Praise Him for His help.
Reader 1:   My soul is cast down within me.

Reader 2:   The LORD will command His loving kindness
                        in the day time,
Reader 1:   and in the night His song shall be with me.
    Choir: My prayer is to the God of my life.
Reader 1:   I will say unto God my rock,
Reader 2:   Why have you forgotten me?
Reader 1:   Why do I mourn because
                        of the oppression of the enemy?
Reader 2:   Mine enemies reproach me.
Reader 1:   They ask me these questions:
Reader 2:   Where is your God?
Reader 1:   Why are you cast down?
Reader 2:   Why are you so distressed?
Audience: Then I will hope in God
    Choir: and I will praise Him.
Reader 1:   Who is the health of my countenance?
Reader 2:   The Lord God is my health and strength!
Reader 1:   This ends the reading.

God Is Our Refuge

Adapted from Psalm 46

Reader 1,2, Audience, Choir

Introduction

Reader 1:   In spite of upheavals of the earth

Reader 2:   this Psalm encourages the church

Reader 1:   to put its confidence in the Most High.

Reader 2:   This Scripture is a promise that the church
             will not be moved.

Reader 1:   And finally we see the intervention

Reader 2:   of God in truth and victory.

Reader 1:   Let us read together Psalm 46.

Psalm 46

Choir: God is our refuge and strength,

Reader 1:   a very present help in trouble.

Audience: Therefore we will not fear,

Reader 2:   though the earth be removed,

Reader 1:   and though the mountains be carried
                into the midst of the sea,

Reader 2:   though the waters thereof roar,

Reader 1:   and though the mountains shake
                with the swelling thereof.

Reader 2:   There is a river, whose streams make glad
                the city of God,

Reader 1:   the holy place of the dwelling of the Most High.

Choir: God is in the midst of her.

Audience: She shall not be moved.

Reader 1:   From the beginning God will help her.

Reader 2:   The heathen raged, the kingdoms were moved.

Reader 1:   He uttered His voice, the earth melted.

Audience: The Lord of hosts is with us,

Reader 1:   the God of Jacob is our refuge.

Choir: Come, behold the works of the Lord,

Reader 2:   what desolations He hath made in the earth.

Reader 1:   He makes wars to cease,

Reader 2:   He breaks the bow,

Reader 1:   and cuts the spear in two.

Reader 2:   He burns the chariot in the fire.

Choir: Be still, and know that I am God.

Reader 1:   I will be exalted among the nations.

Reader 2:   I will be exalted in the earth.

Audience: The Lord of hosts is with us.

Reader 1:   The God of Jacob is our refuge and strength.

Reader 2:   This ends the reading.

A Psalm of Praise to God
Adapted from Psalm 47
Reader 1,2, Audience, Choir

Introduction

Reader 1: The Psalmist worships the Almighty

Reader 2:   by a trumpet, by words of praise.

Reader 1: Let us worship with him together by reading Psalm 47.

Psalm 47

Choir: O clap your hands, all you people:

Audience: shout to God with the voice of triumph.

Reader 1: For the Lord Most High is to be feared.

Reader 2: He is a great King over all the earth.

Reader 1: He shall subdue the people under us,

Reader 2:   and the nations under our feet.

Reader 1: He shall choose our inheritance for us,

Reader 2:   the excellency of Jacob whom he loved.

Reader 1: Announce God with a shout,

Reader 2:   the Lord with the sound of a trumpet.

Audience: Sing praises to God,

Choir: sing honor to our Lord,

Audience: sing praises to our King.

Reader 1: For God is the King of all the earth,

Audience: sing praises with understanding.

Reader 2: God reigns over the heathen.

Reader 1: God sits on the throne of His holiness.

Reader 2: The princes of the people are gathered together,

Reader 1:   even the people of God,

Reader 2:   for the powers of the earth belong unto God.

Reader 1: He is greatly exalted.

Reader 2: This ends the reading.

God Speaks
Adapted from Psalm 50
Reader 1,2, Audience

Introduction

Reader 1: Our reading affirms that
Reader 2:   God is still in control of this world
Reader 1:   and will assert Himself
Reader 2:   as the judge and owner
Reader 1:   of all that lives.
Reader 2: His final words being,
Reader 1:   I will show my salvation.
Reader 2: Join us as we read from Psalm 50.

Psalm 50

Reader 1: The mighty God,
Reader 2:   even the LORD, has spoken,
Reader 1:   and called the earth from the rising of the sun
Reader 2:   to its going down.
Reader 1: Out of Zion, the perfection of beauty,
Audience: God revealed Himself
Reader 2:   and shall not keep silence.
Audience: Our God shall come,
Reader 1:   as a devouring fire.
Reader 2: He shall call from the heavens and the earth,
Reader 1:   that He may judge His people.
Reader 2: Gather my saints together unto me;
Reader 1:   those that have made a covenant with me by sacrifice.
Reader 2: And the heavens shall declare His righteousness.
Audience: God is judge Himself.
Reader 1: Hear, O my people, and I will speak.
Reader 2: I am God, even your God.

Reader 1:   I will not reprove you for your sacrifices
       or burnt offerings.
Audience: For every beast of the forest is mine,
Reader 1:   and the cattle upon a thousand hills.
Reader 2:   I know all the fowls of the mountains,
Reader 1:   and the wild beasts of the field are mine.
Audience: Whoever offers praise glorifies me
Reader 2:   and to him that ordered his conversation aright
Reader 1:   will I show the salvation of God.
Reader 2:   This ends the reading.

David's Prayer of Forgiveness

Adapted from Psalm 51

Reader 1,2, Audience

Introduction

Reader 1: This is a prayer of David

Reader 2:   written after Nathan had confronted him

Reader 1:   concerning his illicit affair with Bathsheba.

Reader 2: You can clearly see that David

Reader 1:   indeed is man after God's own heart.

Reader 2: Join with us in the reading from Psalm 51.

Psalm 51

Reader 1: You desire not sacrifices or burnt offering

Reader 2:   else would I give it.

Reader 1: So have mercy upon me, O God.

Audience: Have mercy upon *us*, O God.

Reader 2: According to your loving kindness and tender mercies,

Reader 1:   blot out my transgressions.

Audience: Please, blot out *our* transgressions.

Reader 1: Wash me thoroughly from my iniquity,

Reader 2:   and cleanse me from my ever present sin.

Reader 1: Against you, you only, have I sinned,

Reader 2:   and done this evil in your sight.

Reader 1: You are right in accusing me

Reader 2:   and justified in passing sentence on me.

Reader 1: I was shaped in iniquity,

Reader 2:   was a sinner from the moment my mother conceived me.

Reader 1: Purge me with mint,

Reader 2:   and I shall be clean,

Reader 1:   wash me,

Reader 2:   and I shall be whiter than snow.

Audience: And we **shall** be whiter than snow.

Reader 1: Make me to hear joy and gladness.

Reader 2: Hide your face from my sins,

Reader 1:   and blot out all my iniquities.

Reader 2: Create in me a clean heart, O God,

Reader 1:   renew a right spirit within me,

Audience: and a right spirit within **us**!

Reader 1: Cast me not away from your presence

Reader 2:   and take not your holy spirit from me.

Reader 1: Restore unto me the joy of your salvation.

Audience: Restore unto **us** the joy of your salvation.

Reader 2: Uphold me with your spirit,

Reader 1:   then will we teach transgressors your ways

Reader 2:   and sinners shall be converted.

Reader 1: Deliver me from blood guiltiness,

Audience: You, God, is my salvation.

Reader 2: I will sing aloud of your righteousness.

Audience: O Lord, **we** shall sing your praises.

Reader 1: You desire not sacrifices or burnt offering,

Reader 2:   else would I give it.

Reader 1: The sacrifices of God are a broken spirit.

Reader 2: Do not despise my broken and contrite heart.

Reader 1: Show your good pleasure to Zion,

Reader 2:   build the walls of Jerusalem.

Reader 1: Then you will be pleased with the sacrifices of righteousness.

There is no God
Adapted from Psalm 53
Readers 1,2, Choir

Introduction

Reader 1: The Psalmist shows in this reading
just how bad we are,

Reader 2: how utterly devoid of any goodness,

Reader 1: and that none do good.

Reader 2: The results of doing evil is given,

Reader 1: but there is salvation!

Reader 2: Let us read together Psalm 53.

Psalm 53

Reader 1: The fool has said in his heart,

Choir: there is no God.

Reader 2: They are evil.

Reader 1: They practice abominable iniquities.

Reader 2: There are none that do good.

Choir: God looks down from heaven

Reader 1: on the children of men,

Reader 2: to see if there were any that did understand,

Reader 1: or see if there were any that did seek Him.

Reader 2: Every one of them has turned their backs on God.

Reader 1: They are altogether become corrupt.

Choir: There are none that do good, no, not one.

Reader 2: Have the workers of iniquity no knowledge

Reader 1: who eat up my people as they eat bread?

Reader 2: They have not called upon God.

Reader 1: They were in great fear,

Reader 2: where there was nothing to fear.

Reader 1: God has scattered the bones of them
who assault them,

Reader 2:   those who put them to shame,
Reader 1:   because God has despised them.
Reader 2:   Oh that the salvation of Israel
                    were come out of Zion!
Reader 1:   When God brings back the captivity of his people,
    Choir: Jacob and Israel shall rejoice and be glad!
Reader 2:   This ends the reading.

God Listens to Our Vows
Adapted from Psalm 61
Readers 1,2, Choir

Introduction

Reader 1: David successfully pleads with the Lord
Reader 2:   to be sheltered in His care.
Reader 1: David promises to trust
Reader 2:   in the God of mercy and truth.
Reader 1: Let us read together Psalm 61.

Psalm 61

Reader 1: Hear my cry, O God!
Choir: Listen to my prayer.
Reader 1: From the end of the earth will I cry to you
Reader 2:   when my heart is overwhelmed, then,
Choir: lead me to the rock that is higher than I.
Reader 1: For you have been a shelter for me
Reader 2:   and a strong tower from the enemy.
Choir: I will abide in your house forever.
Reader 1: I will trust in the shelter of your wings.
Reader 2: For you, O God, have heard my promises.
Reader 1: You have given me the heritage of those
        who fear your name.
Choir: You will lengthen my life
Reader 2:   and his years as many generations.
Reader 1: I will abide before God forever.
Reader 2: Let mercy and truth preserve me.
Choir: So will I sing praise to your name forever,
Reader 1:   that I may daily perform my vows and promises.
Reader 2: This ends the reading.

Waiting Is Worth It

Adapted from Psalm 62
Reader 1,2, Audience, Choir

Introduction

Reader 1: The reading is an affirmation

Reader 2:   of the Lord's presence

Reader 1:   for those who put their confidence in Him.

Reader 2: The least and greatest of people without God

Reader 1:   are counted as nothing.

Reader 2: Join with us in the reading taken from Psalm 62.

Psalm 62

Reader 1: My soul waits on God,

Reader 2:   from Him comes my salvation.

Choir: He only is my rock,

Audience: my salvation,

Choir: my defense,

Reader 1:   therefore I shall not be greatly moved.

Reader 2: How long will you imagine mischief against a person?

Reader 1: Will all be killed

Reader 2:   as a leaning wall or tottering fence?

Reader 1: They only consult to destroy from his excellency.

Reader 2: They delight in lies.

Reader 1: They bless with their mouth,

Reader 2:   but they curse inwardly.

Audience: My soul waits only on God,

Reader 2:   for my expectation is from Him.

Choir: He only is my rock,

Audience: my salvation,

Choir: my defense.

Audience: I shall not be moved.

Reader 1: In God is my salvation and my glory,

Reader 2:	the rock of my strength, and my refuge.
Audience:	Trust in Him at all times.
Reader 1:	Pour out your heart before Him
Choir:	because God is a refuge for us.
Reader 2:	Surely the least of people are vane
Reader 1:	and the greatest of people are a lie.
Reader 2:	When laid in a balance they are lighter than a breath.
Reader 1:	Trust not in oppression
Reader 2:	and become not vain in robbery.
Reader 1:	If riches increase, set not your heart on them.
Reader 2:	God has spoken once,
Reader 1:	twice have I heard this;
Choir:	that power belongs to God.
Audience:	To you, O Lord, belongs mercy;
Reader 2:	you render to every man according to his work.

Seeking and Trusting God

Adapted from Psalm 63
Readers 1,2

Introduction

Reader 1: This is a Psalm of David

Reader 2:   when he was in the wilderness of Judah.

Reader 1: He expresses his devotion

Reader 2:   to the God who sustains him.

Reader 1: Listen now to the reading of Psalm 63.

Psalm 63

Reader 1: O God, you are my God.

Reader 2: Early will I seek you.

Reader 1: My soul thirsts for you,

Reader 2:   my flesh longs for you in a dry and thirsty land.

Reader 1: I have seen your power and your glory in the sanctuary.

Reader 2: Because your loving kindness is better than life,

Reader 1:   my lips shall praise you.

Reader 2: Thus I will bless you while I live.

Reader 1: I will lift up my hands in your name.

Reader 2: My flesh shall be satisfied

Reader 1:   as with marrow and fatness.

Reader 2: My mouth shall praise you with joyful lips.

Reader 1: I remember you on my bed,

Reader 2:   and meditate on you in the night watches.

Reader 1: Because you have been my help,

Reader 2:   therefore in the shadow of your wings will I rejoice.

Reader 1: My flesh followed hard after you.

Reader 2: Your right hand upholds me.

Reader 1: But those that seek my life to destroy it,

Reader.2:   shall go into the lower parts of the earth.

Reader 1: They shall fall by the sword.

Reader 2:   They shall be a portion for foxes.
Reader 1:   But I the king shall rejoice in God.
Reader 2:   Every one that swears by Him shall be glorified.
Reader 1:   But the mouth of them that speak lies shall be stopped.
Reader 2:   This ends the reading.

Hymn of Thanksgiving
Adapted from Psalm 65
Readers 1,2, Choir

Introduction

Reader 1: A Psalm and song of David,

Reader 2: a hymn of thanksgiving

Reader 1: acknowledging the God who cares for us spiritually

Reader 2: and prepares the earth for grain to grow.

Reader 1: Listen as we read together Psalm 65.

Psalm 65

Reader 1: Praise waits for you, O God,

Reader 2: and to you shall the vow be performed.

Choir: O you who hears prayers,

Reader 1: to you shall all people come.

Reader 2: Iniquities prevail against me.

Reader 1: As for our transgressions

Reader 2: you shall purge them away.

Choir: Blessed is the person whom you choose

Reader 1: to dwell in your courts. We shall be satisfied

Reader 2: with the goodness of your house.

Reader 1: In righteousness will you answer us.

Choir: O God of our salvation,

Reader 2: you are the confidence of all the ends of the earth

Reader 1: and of them that are afar off upon the sea.

Choir: By your strength you set fast the mountains,

Reader 1: stilled the noises of the seas and their waves,

Reader 2: and quieted the tumult of the people.

Reader 1: They that dwell in all the earth

Reader 2: are in awe of your creation.

Choir: You make the mornings and evenings a time to rejoice.

Reader 1: You visit the earth to water it.

Reader 2:   You greatly enrich it with the river of God,

Reader 1:   which is full of water

Reader 2:   that causes corn to grow.

Reader 1:   You abundantly water the ridges.

Reader 2:   You set the furrows.

Reader 1:   You make the earth soft with showers.

Reader 2:   You bless the springs.

   Choir: You crown the year with your goodness

Reader 1:   and your paths drop fatness.

Reader 2:   They drop upon the pastures of the wilderness

Reader 1:   and the little hills rejoice on every side.

Reader 2:   The pastures are clothed with flocks.

Reader 1:   The valleys also are covered over with corn.

Reader 2:   They shout for joy, they also sing.

   Choir: Praise waits for you, O God.

Reader 1: Amen.

Prayer for the Kingdom
Adapted from Psalm 67
Reader 1,2, Audience, Choir

Introduction
Reader 1: This Psalm is a tribute
Reader 2:   to God's willingness
Reader 1:   to fill us with good health and happiness.
Reader 2: Let us join David as we read together Psalm 67.

Psalm 67
Reader 1: God be merciful to us
Audience: and bless us
Choir: and cause your face to shine upon us:
Reader 2: That your way may be known on earth,
Reader 1:   your saving health among all nations.
Choir: Let us praise you, O God.
Audience: Let all the people praise you.
Reader 2: O let the nations be glad and sing for joy:
Reader 1:   for you shall judge the people righteously
Reader 2:   and govern the nations upon earth.
Audience: Let us praise you, O God.
Choir: Let all the people praise you.
Reader 1: Then shall the earth yield her increase
Reader 2:   and God, even our own God, shall bless us.
Reader 1: God shall bless us
Reader 2:   and all the ends of the earth shall fear Him.
Audience: God be merciful to us.
Reader 1: Amen.

O God You Are My Confidence

Adapted from Psalm 71
Reader 1,2, Audience, Choir

Introduction

Reader 1:　David recounts how God has been with him

Reader 2:　　from his birth until old age.

Reader 1:　He praises God in spite of those

Reader 2:　　who would do him in.

Reader 1:　And now let us read together

Reader 2:　　as David praises God from Psalm 71.

Psalm 71

Reader 1:　In you, O Lord, do I put my trust.

Reader 2:　In your righteousness

Audience:　　deliver me,

Choir:　　listen to me,

Audience:　　save me.

Reader 2:　In your strong habitation

Audience:　　shelter me

Reader 1:　　with the rock of salvation.

Reader 2:　Lord, deliver me from the hand of the wicked.

Reader 1:　Shelter me from the grasp of the cruel.

Audience:　O Lord God, you are my trust,

Reader 2:　　from the day I was born

Reader 1:　　and from my youth

Audience:　　you are my confidence.

Reader 1:　Let my mouth be filled with your praises,

Reader 2:　　that others may see

Choir:　　you are my strong refuge.

Reader 1:　Then when I am old

Reader 2:　　and my strength fails

Choir:　　cast me not off.

Reader 1:   Even when my enemies say,

Choir: God has forsaken me.

Reader 2:   O Lord God, be not far from me.

Reader 1:   Confound and consume my adversaries,

Reader 2:   cover them with reproach and shame.

Reader 1:   However, as for me,

Choir: I will hope forever,

Audience: praising you more and more.

Reader 1:   I will speak of your righteousness

Reader 2:   and salvation days without end.

Reader 1:   O Lord God, you have taught me

Reader 2:   from my youth, and from this day,

Audience: I will declare your wonderful works.

Reader 1:   Now I am old and grey headed,

Audience: O Lord God, do not forsake me,

Reader 2:   until, until,

Audience: I have shown your power

Reader 2:   to this generation.

Reader 1:   Because you have brought shame

Reader 2:   to those who seek my harm

Choir: I will praise you with music.

Audience: My lips will sing your praises.

Reader 1:   My tongue will talk of your righteousness.

Reader 2:   O Lord God, you are the Holy One of Israel.

Reader 1:   This ends the reading.

Prayers for Solomon by David

Adapted from Psalm 72

Readers 1,2,3

Introduction

Reader 1: David prays for Solomon his son

Reader 2:   and soon to be king.

Reader 1: Then David describes the glories of Solomon's reign.

Reader 2: As usual for David, this Psalm gives praise to God.

Reader 1: Listen as we read Psalm 72.

Psalm 72

Reader 3: Give the king your judgments, O God,

Reader 2:   and your righteousness to the king's son.

Reader 3: He shall judge your people with righteousness

Reader 1:   and your poor with judgment.

Reader 2: The mountains shall bring peace to the people

Reader 1:   and the little hills, by righteousness.

Reader 3: He shall judge the poor of the people.

Reader 2: He shall save the children of the needy

Reader 1:   and shall break in pieces the oppressor.

Reader 2: They shall fear you as long as the sun and moon endure.

Reader 3: He shall come down like rain

Reader 1:   on the mown grass

Reader 2:   as showers that water the earth.

Reader 1: In his days shall the righteous flourish

Reader 2:   and abundance of peace so long as the moon endures.

Reader 3: He shall have dominion also from sea to sea

Reader 1:   and from the river to the ends of the earth.

Reader 2: They that dwell in the wilderness shall bow before him

Reader 1:   and his enemies shall lick the dust.

Reader 2: Kings shall offer him gifts.

Reader 1: All kings shall fall down before him.

Reader 2:   All nations shall serve him.

Reader 1:   He shall deliver the poor and needy,

Reader 2:   who have no helper, when they cry.

Reader 3:   He shall spare the poor and needy,

Reader 2:   and shall save the souls of the needy.

Reader 3:   He shall redeem their soul from deceit and violence.
And he shall live daily to be praised

Reader 1:   with gold and continual prayers.

Reader 2:   Corn and grass will flourish throughout the earth.

Reader 3:   His name shall endure forever as long as the sun shines.

Reader 1:   Men will be blessed in him

Reader 2:   and all nations shall call him blessed.

Reader 3:   Blessed be the Lord God, the God of Israel,
who only does wondrous things.

Reader 1:   And blessed be his glorious name for ever

Reader 2:   and let the whole earth be filled with his glory.

Reader 1:   Amen, and Amen.

Reader 3:   The prayers of David for Solomon are ended.

Why the Wicked Prosper
Adapted from Psalm 73
Readers 1,2,3,4

Introduction

Reader 1:   David has great concern that the wicked
Reader 2:   seem to have it all together
Reader 3:   while the righteous suffer and go hungry.
Reader 4:   Perhaps some of these thoughts
                have crossed your mind
Reader 1:   as you walk the Christian pathway.
Reader 2:   Here is David's rationale as to why he seeks God.
Reader 3:   The reading is taken from Psalm 73.

Psalm 73

Reader 1:   Truly God is good to Israel,
Reader 2:   even to such as are of a clean heart.
Reader 1:   But as for me, my feet had almost stumbled.
Reader 2:   My steps had well-nigh slipped.
Reader 1:   For I was envious at the foolish,
Reader 2:   when I saw the prosperity of the wicked.
Reader 3:   For there is no pain in their death,
Reader 4:   but their strength is firm.
Reader 3:   They are not in trouble as other men,
Reader 4:   neither are they plagued like others.
Reader 3:   Pride is as a chain around their neck.
Reader 4:   Violence covers them as a garment.
Reader 3:   Their eyes stand out with fatness.
Reader 4:   They have more than the heart could wish.
Reader 3:   They are corrupt, and speak wickedly
                concerning oppression.
Reader 4:   They set their mouth against the heavens
Reader 3:   and their tongues walk through the earth.

Reader 4:   And they say, How does God know?

Reader 3:   Is there knowledge in the most High?

Reader 1:   Behold, these are the ungodly,

Reader 2:   who prosper and increase riches in the world.

Reader 1:   Now I have cleansed my heart in vain

Reader 2:   and washed my hands in innocence.

Reader 1:   For all the daylong have I been plagued

Reader 2:   and every morning I have been punished.

Reader 1:   If I will speak as the wicked speak,

Reader 2:   I would offend the generation of your children.

Reader 1:   When I thought to know this,

Reader 2:   it was too painful for me

Reader 1:   until I went into the sanctuary of God;

Reader 2:   then I understood their end.

Reader 3:   You did set them in slippery places.

Reader 4:   You cast them down into destruction.

Reader 3:   How are they brought into desolation?

Reader 4:   In a moment they are utterly consumed with terrors,

Reader 3:   as a dream when one awakes.

Reader 1:   So foolish was I, and ignorant.

Reader 2:   Nevertheless I am continually with you.

Reader 1:   You have held me by my right hand.

Reader 2:   You will guide me with your counsel,
      and afterward receive me to glory.

Reader 1:   Whom do I have in heaven but you?

Reader 2:   There is none upon earth that I desire beside you.

Reader 1:   My flesh and my heart fail.

Reader 2:   But God is the strength of my heart,
      and my portion forever.

Reader 1:   It is good for me to draw near to God.

Reader 2:   I have put my trust in the Lord GOD,

Reader 1:   that I may declare all his works.

Reader 2:   This ends the reading.

Troubles, Temptation, Encouragement
Adapted from Psalm 77
Reader 1,2, Audience, Choir

Introduction
Reader 1:   This reading recalls the writer's
            troubles and temptations.
Reader 2:   In spite of problems
Reader 1:   he finds encouragement in remembering
Reader 2:   how God has helped his people.
Reader 1:   The last few verses are symbolically crafted to
            emphasize the power of God.
Reader 2:   Let us join together in reading Psalm 77.

Psalm 77
Reader 1:   I cried to God with my voice
Reader 2:   and He heard me.
Reader 1:   In the day of my trouble I sought the Lord.
Reader 2:   My pain ran in the night, and ceased not.
Reader 1:   My soul refused to be comforted.
Audience: I remembered God, and was troubled.
Reader 2:   I complained and my spirit was overwhelmed.
Audience: I could not sleep.
Choir: I am so troubled that I could not speak.
Reader 1:   I have considered the days of old,
Reader 2:   the years of ancient times.
Choir: I remembered my song in the night.
Audience: I commune with my own heart
Reader 1:   and my spirit made diligent search.
Choir: Will the Lord cast off forever?
Audience: Will he be favorable no more?
Reader 2:   Is his mercy gone forever?
Reader 1:   Does his promise fail for evermore?

Audience:	Has God forgotten to be gracious?
Choir:	Has he in anger shut up his tender mercies?
Reader 1:	And I said, This is my infirmity.
Reader 2:	I will remember the years of the right hand of the most High.
Audience:	I will remember the works of the LORD.
Reader 1:	Surely I will remember your wonders of old.
Reader 2:	I will meditate on all your work
Reader 1:	and talk of your doings.
Reader 2:	Your way, O God, is in the sanctuary.
Audience:	Who is so great as our God?
Choir:	You are the God that does wonders.
Reader 1:	You have declared your strength among the people.
Reader 2:	You have with your arm redeemed your people.
Reader 1:	O God, the waters saw you!
Reader 2:	They were afraid
Reader 1:	and the depths also were troubled.
Reader 2:	The clouds poured out water and the skies sent out a sound.
Reader 1:	The voice of your thunder was in the heaven.
Reader 2:	The lightning lightened the world.
Reader 1:	The earth trembled and shook.
Reader 2:	Your way is in the sea,
Reader 1:	and your path in the great waters,
Reader 2:	and your footsteps are not known.
Audience:	You led your people like a flock
Reader 1:	by the hand of Moses and Aaron.
Reader 2:	This ends the reading.

A Wayward People

Adapted from 78 (1st part)

Readers 1,2, Choir

Introduction

Reader 1: The reading gives a wonderful account

Reader 2:   of God's miraculous dealing with the children of Israel,

Reader 1:   but a dismal account of their response.

Reader 2: In the end God does forgive them.

Reader 1: So we, too, can take heart in knowing

Reader 2:   that God loves us in spite of ourselves.

Reader 1: Listen as part one of Psalm 78 is read.

Psalm 78 (1st part)

Choir: Give ear, O my people, to my law

Reader 1:   incline your ears to the words of my mouth,

Reader 2:   which we have heard and known,

Reader 1:   and our fathers have told us.

Reader 2: We will not hide them from their children,

Reader 1:   showing to the generation to come
    the praises of the LORD,

Reader 2:   and his strength,

Reader 1:   and his wonderful works that he hath done.

Choir: He commanded our fathers,

Reader 2:   that they should make them known to their children,

Reader 1:   so that the generation to come might know them,

Choir: that they might set their hope in God,

Reader 2:   and not forget His works,

Reader 1:   but keep his commandments.

Choir: But, not be as their fathers,

Reader 2:   a stubborn and rebellious generation

Reader 1:   and whose spirit was not steadfast with God.

Choir: They forgot his works,

Reader 2:   and his marvelous things he did

Reader 1:   in the sight of their fathers, in the land of Egypt.

Choir: He divided the sea,

Reader 2:   and caused them to pass through.

Reader 1:   In the daytime he led them with a cloud,

Reader 2:   and at night with a light of fire.

Choir: He brought streams out of the rock,

Reader 1:   and caused waters to run down like rivers.

Choir: Yet they sinned more against him,

Reader 2:   provoking the most High in the wilderness,

Reader 1:   by asking meat for their lust.

Reader 2:   They spoke against God, saying,

Choir: Can God furnish a table in the wilderness?

Reader 2:   Behold, He smote the rock

Reader 1:   and waters gushed out.

Choir: Can He give bread also?

Reader 1:   The LORD heard this and was angry

Reader 2:   because they believed not in Him

Reader 1:   and trusted not in His salvation.

Choir: God rained down manna for them to eat.

Reader 2:   They ate angel's food to the full!

Reader 1:   He rained flesh upon them as dust

Reader 2:   and feathered fowls like as the sand of the sea.

Choir: So they did eat, and were well filled;

Reader 1:   he gave them their own desire.

Reader 2:   But while their meat was yet in their mouths,

Reader 1:   the wrath of God came upon them,

Reader 2:   and He killed the chosen men of Israel.

Reader 1:   After all this they sinned still

Reader 2:   and believed not for his wondrous works.

Reader 1:   When he killed them,

Choir: then they sought him

Reader 2:   and they returned and enquired early after God.

Choir: They remembered that God was their rock

Reader 2:   and the high God, their redeemer.

Reader 1:   Nevertheless they did flatter him with their mouth,

Reader 2:   and they lied to him with their tongues.

Reader 1:   For their heart was not right with Him,

Reader 2:   neither were they steadfast in His covenant.

Choir: But He, being full of compassion,

Reader 1:   forgave their iniquity,

Reader 2:   and destroyed them not.

Reader 1:   Yet many a time turned He his anger away.

Reader 2:   For He remembered that they were but flesh,

Reader 1:   as a wind that passes away and does not return.

Reader 2:   This ends the reading.

Rescued and Ungrateful

Adapted from 78 (2nd part)

Readers 1,2, Choir

Introduction

Reader 1: The Psalmist recounts the plagues of Egypt

Reader 2:   and how the Israelites were saved and protected.

Reader 1: Unfortunately the story does not end there

Reader 2:   as the Israelites were not faithful

Reader 1:   to the one who rescued them.

Reader 2: Listen as we read the second part of Psalm 78.

Psalm 78 (2nd part)

Reader 2: How often did they provoke him in the wilderness,

Reader 1:   and grieve him in the desert!

Reader 2: They turned their backs and tempted God,

Reader 1:   and limited the Holy One of Israel.

Choir: They remembered not his hand,

Reader 2:   nor the day when he delivered them from the enemy.

Reader 1: How did He show his signs in Egypt?

Reader 2: He turned their rivers into blood

Reader 1:   so that they could not drink.

Reader 2: He sent many sorts of flies among them,
which devoured them,

Reader 1:   and frogs, which destroyed them.

Reader 2: He gave also their increase to the caterpillar

Reader 1:   and their labor to the locust.

Choir: He destroyed their vines with hail

Reader 2:   and their sycamore trees with frost.

Reader 1: He gave up their cattle to the hail

Reader 2:   and their flocks to hot thunderbolts.

Reader 1: He cast upon them the fierceness of his anger

Reader 2:   by sending evil angels among them.

Choir: He spared not their soul from death,

Reader 2:   but gave their life over to the pestilence.

Choir: He smote all the firstborn in Egypt,

Reader 1:   but made his own people to go forth like sheep

Reader 2:   and guided them in the wilderness like a flock.

Choir: And he led them on safely,

Reader 1:   so that they feared not,

Reader 2:   but the sea overwhelmed their enemies.

Reader 1:   And he brought them to the border of his sanctuary,

Reader 2:   even to this mountain, which
             his right hand had purchased.

Choir: He cast out the heathen before them

Reader 1:   and made the tribes of Israel to dwell in their tents.

Reader 2:   Yet they tempted and provoked the most high God

Reader 1:   and kept not his testimonies.

Reader 2:   They dealt unfaithfully like their fathers.

Reader 1:   They were turned aside like a deceitful bow.

Choir: They provoked him to anger with their high places

Reader 2:   and moved him to jealousy with their graven images.

Reader 1:   When God heard this, he was angry

Reader 2:   and greatly abhorred Israel.

Reader 1:   He delivered his glory into the enemy's hand.

Choir: He gave His people over to the sword

Reader 2:   and was angry with His inheritance.

Reader 1:   The fire consumed their young men

Reader 2:   and their maidens were not given to marriage.

Choir: Their priests fell by the sword

Reader 1:   and their widows made no lamentation.

Reader 2:   Then the LORD awaked as one out of sleep,

Choir: chose David to lead his people.

Reader 1:   He fed them according to the integrity of his heart

Reader 2:   and guided them by the skillfulness of his hands.

Reader 1:   This ends the reading.

Praise and Obligations

Adapted from Psalm 81
Reader 1,2, Audience, Choir

Introduction

Reader 2: In the first part of this chapter God is praised,

Reader 1:   for doing so much for his people.

Reader 2: The last part of this chapter

Reader 1:   tells about their obligations to God.

Reader 2: Let us join together in reading from Psalm 81.

Psalm 81

Reader 1: Rejoice out loud to God, our strength!

Reader 2: Take up a song, strike the drum, play the harp.

Choir: Blow the horn on the new moon,

Reader 2:   at the full moon, for our day of celebration!

Choir: Because this is the law for Israel:

Reader 2:   His is a rule of Jacob's God.

Reader 1: He made it a decree for Joseph

Reader 2:   when he went out from the land of Egypt.

Reader 1: He lifted the burden off your shoulders

Reader 2:   and freed your hands of the brick basket.

Reader 1: In distress you cried out, so I rescued you.

Reader 2: I answered you in the secret of thunder.

Reader 1: I tested you at the waters of Meribah.

Choir: Listen, my people, I'm warning you!

Audience: If only you would listen to me.

Reader 1: There must be no foreign god among you.

Reader 2: You must not bow down to any strange deity.

Choir: I am the LORD your God,

Reader 1:   who brought you up from Egypt's land.

Choir: Open your mouth wide—

Audience: I will fill it up!

Reader 2:   But my people wouldn't listen to my voice.

Reader 1:   Israel simply wasn't agreeable toward me.

Reader 2:   So I sent them off to follow their willful hearts.

Reader 1:   They followed their own advice.

Audience: How I wish my people would listen to me!

Choir: How I wish Israel would walk in my ways!

Reader 2:   Then I would subdue their enemies in a second.

Reader 1:   I would turn my hand against their foes.

Reader 2:   Those who hate the LORD would grovel before me,

Reader 1:   and their doom would last forever!

Reader 2:   But I would feed you with the finest wheat.

Reader 1:   I would satisfy you with honey from the rock.

Reader 2:   This ends the reading.

The Longings of a Soul

Adapted from Psalm 84
Reader 1,2, Audience, Choir

Introduction

Reader 1:   This particular Psalm can scarcely

Reader 2:   be read without hearing the music.

Reader 1:   Listen as the author

Reader 2:   gives heartfelt testimony to be with God.

Reader 1:   Join with us as we read together Psalm 84.

Psalm 84

Reader 1:   How lovely are your tabernacles,

Reader 2:   O LORD of hosts!

Choir: My soul longs, even faints for the courts of the LORD.

Audience: My heart and my flesh cry out for the living God.

Reader 1:   Yea, the sparrow has found a house

Reader 2:   and the swallow a nest for herself,

Reader 1:   where she may lay her young, even your altars,

Reader 2:   O LORD, my King, and my God.

Choir: Blessed are they that dwell in your house:

Audience: they will be still praising you.

Choir: Blessed is the person whose strength is in you,

Reader 2:   in whose heart are the ways of them.

Reader 1:   They go from strength to strength,

Reader 2:   every one of them in Zion appears before God.

Audience: O LORD, hear my prayer.

Reader 1:   Give ear, O God of Jacob.

Choir: Behold, O God our shield,

Reader 2:   look upon the face of your anointed.

Reader 1:   For a day in you courts is better than a thousand.

Audience: I had rather be a doorkeeper in the house of my God,

Choir: than to dwell in the tents of wickedness.

Reader 2:   For the LORD God is a sun and shield.
Audience: The LORD will give grace and glory.
Reader 1:   No good thing will he withhold
             from them who walk uprightly.
Reader 2:   O LORD of hosts,
Reader 1:   blessed is the person who trusts in you.

Mercy and Promise
Adapted from Psalm 85
Reader 1,2, Audience, Choir

Introduction

Reader 1: The reading recounts all the mercy

Reader 2:   God has shown his people

Reader 1:   in spite of their many sins.

Reader 2: Finally, a wonderful promise is given.

Reader 1: Join us in reading of mercy and promise in Psalm 85.

Psalm 85

Reader 1: Lord, you have been favorable to your land.

Reader 2: You have forgiven the iniquity of your people.

Audience: You have covered all their sins.

Choir: You have taken away your wrath.

Reader 1: You have turned yourself
from the fierceness of your anger.

Reader 2: Turn us, O God of our salvation,

Reader 1:   and cause your anger toward us to cease.

Choir: Will you be angry with us forever?

Reader 2: Will you draw out your anger to all generations?

Audience: Will you not revive us again

Reader 1:   that your people may rejoice in you?

Audience: Show us your mercy, O LORD,

Choir: and grant us your salvation.

Reader 2: I will hear what God says:

Reader 1:   for he will speak peace to his people, his saints.

Reader 2: But let them not turn again to folly.

Choir: His salvation is near to them that fear him;

Reader 1:   that glory may dwell in our land.

Reader 2: Mercy and truth are met together.

Audience: Righteousness and peace have kissed each other.

Reader 1:   Truth shall spring out of the earth

Reader 2:   and righteousness shall look down from heaven.

Choir: The Lord shall give that which is good

Reader 1:   and our land shall yield her increase.

Reader 2:   Righteousness shall go before him

Reader 1:   and shall set us in the way of his steps.

Reader 2:   This ends the reading.

God of Mercy
Adapted from Psalm 86
Reader 1,2, Audience, Choir

Introduction

Reader 1: The Psalmist holds a conversation with God
Reader 2: telling him to hear his prayer
Reader 1: because he is in great need
Reader 2: and that he needs to be taught
the ways of righteousness.
Reader 1: In spite of the difficulties the Psalmist encounters
Reader 2: he glorifies God because he has been delivered.
Reader 1: Let us read together Psalm 86.

Psalm 86

Reader 1: O God,
Audience: the Lord God of all creation
Reader 2: bow down your ear,
Reader 1: hear me,
Reader 2: preserve my soul,
Reader 1: save your servant.
Audience: Be merciful unto me, O Lord:
Reader 1: for I am poor and needy,
Reader 2: for I am holy,
Reader 1: for I cry unto you daily,
Audience: for I trust in you.
Choir: O my Lord, you have saved my life
Reader 2: because you are good,
Reader 1: ready to forgive,
Reader 2: abundant in mercy,
Reader 1: listening to my prayers.
Reader 2: In the day of my trouble

Audience:	I will call upon you
Choir:	and I will answer you.
Reader 2:	Among the gods there is none like you.
Reader 1:	There are no works like your works.
Audience:	You have made all nations
Reader 2:	and they will worship before you
Reader 1:	and glorify you name.
Choir:	I am God alone.
Reader 2:	You are great
Reader 1:	and do wondrous things:
Audience:	Teach me your way, O LORD:
Choir:	I will walk in truth.
Reader 2:	I will fear your name
Reader 1:	and praise you with all my heart.
Audience:	I will glorify your name forevermore.
Reader 2:	O God, for great is your mercy toward me.
Reader 1:	You have delivered my soul from the lowest hell.
Choir:	The proud are risen against me.
Reader 2:	Many violent men have sought to destroy my soul.
Audience:	But you, O Lord, are a God full of compassion,
Reader 1:	gracious,
Reader 2:	long suffering,
Reader 1:	and abundant in mercy and truth.
Audience:	Have mercy upon me.
Reader 2:	Give strength to your servant.
Reader 1:	Because you show me a token for good,
Reader 2:	they who hate me shall see it, and be ashamed,
Choir:	I will hold you and comfort you.
Reader 1:	Thanks be to God for these words.

Lord, Our Dwelling Place

Adapted from Psalm 90
Reader 1,2, Audience, Choir

Introduction

Reader 1: The Psalmist extols the safety

Reader 2:   in being in the presence of an omnipotent being,

Reader 1:   while realizing his frailties

Reader 2:   and the shortness of his life.

Reader 1: He concludes with an appeal to God

Reader 2:   to help him number his days.

Reader 1: Let us read together Psalm 90.

Psalm 90

Reader 1: Lord, you have been our dwelling place,

Audience: truly a place of comfort,

Reader 2:   in all generations.

Audience: Before the mountains were created,

Reader 1:   or before you formed the earth and the world,

Reader 2:   even from everlasting to everlasting,

Choir: you are God.

Reader 1: For you a thousand years are but as yesterday

Reader 2:   or as a few hours in the night.

Reader 1: You carry them away as with a flood.

Choir: They sleep,

Reader 2:   but in the morning they are like new grass,

Reader 1:   which flourishes and grows,

Reader 2:   then in the evening it is cut down and dies.

Audience: We are consumed by your anger.

Choir: We fear for your wrath.

Audience: It troubles us!

Reader 2: You have set our iniquities before you.

Reader 1: To you our secret sins are secret no more.

Reader 2:   For all our days are passed away in your wrath.

Audience: We spend our years as a tale that is told.

Reader 2:   The days of our years are threescore years and ten

Reader 1:   and perhaps fourscore years if we have the strength.

Audience: Those years are filled with labor and sorrow.

Reader 1:   All too soon the years are gone

Reader 2:   and we fly away.

Choir: According to your fear, so is your wrath.

Reader 1:   Who can understand it?

Reader 2:   So teach us to number our days,

Reader 1:   that we may apply our hearts unto wisdom.

Choir: Return, O Lord, how long?

Audience: Repent of your anger toward us.

Reader 1:   In the morning

Audience: satisfy us early with your mercy.

Reader 1:   In the evening

Audience: make us glad.

Reader 1:   Make us glad for as many days as you afflicted us.

Reader 2:   Make us glad

Reader 1:   for as many years as we have seen evil.

Choir: Let your work appear unto your servants,

Reader 2:   and your glory to their children.

Audience: Let the beauty of the Lord be upon us.

Choir: Establish the work of your hands.

Reader 2:   Yes, establish *in us* the work of your hands.

Reader 1:   This ends the reading.

Under His Shadow
Adapted from Psalm 91
Reader 1,2, Audience, Choir

Introduction

Reader 1:	Our reading for today
Reader 2:	is probably the most read Psalm
Reader 1:	when the world around us
Reader 2:	provides no hope or escape.
Reader 1:	Let us read together Psalm 91
Reader 2:	for much needed comfort and strength.

Psalm 91

Reader 1:	He that dwells in the secret place of the most High
Reader 2:	shall abide under the shadow of the Almighty.
Reader 1:	I will say of the LORD,
Audience:	He is our refuge and our fortress,
Choir:	our God, in him will we trust.
Reader 1:	He will save you from the snare of the fowler,
Reader 2:	and from the deadly pestilence.
Reader 1:	He shall cover you with his feathers,
Reader 2:	and under his wings shall you will be safe.
Audience:	His truth shall be our shield.
Choir:	Fear not the terror by night,
Reader 2:	nor for the arrow that flies by day,
Reader 1:	nor for the pestilence that appears in darkness,
Reader 2:	nor for the destruction that awaits at noonday.
Audience:	A thousand shall fall at our side,
Choir:	and ten thousand at our right hand,
Reader 1:	but it shall not come close to you.
Reader 2:	With your eyes shall you see the reward of the wicked,
Reader 1:	because you have made the LORD, your habitation.

Audience:	There shall no evil befall us,
Choir:	neither shall any plague come near us.
Reader 2:	For he shall give his angels charge over you,
Reader 1:	to keep you in all your ways.
Reader 2:	even your foot from dashing against a stone.
Reader 1:	You shall step on the lion and adder.
Reader 2:	The dragon shall you trample under foot.
Audience:	Because he has set his love upon us,
Reader 1:	then He will deliver us.
Choir:	We will set him on high,
Reader 2:	because he knows your name.
Audience:	The Lord will call upon us,
Reader 1:	and He will answer.
Choir:	He will be with us in trouble.
Reader 2:	To honor him
Reader 1:	with long life will I satisfy him
Reader 2:	and show him my salvation.

Praise Everywhere
Adapted from Psalm 92
Reader 1,2, Audience, Choir

Introduction
Reader 1: The writer of Psalm 92 gives the Lord
Reader 2:   honor and praise with music and voice.
Reader 1: He acknowledges that the wicked do prosper
Reader 2:   but their end is destruction
Reader 1:   while the righteous are fruitful to the end.
Reader 2: Let us read together this Psalm 92.

Psalm 92
Choir: It is a good thing to give thanks to you LORD
Reader 1:   and to sing praises to your name.
Audience: To show your loving kindness in the morning,
Reader 2:   your faithfulness every night
Reader 1:   on the harp with a solemn sound.
Reader 2: For you, LORD,
Reader 1:   have made me glad through your work.
Reader 2: I will triumph in the works of your hands.
Audience: O LORD, how great are your works!
Reader 2: Your thoughts are very deep.
Choir: A fool does not understand this.
Reader 1: While the wicked spring up as grass and flourish,
Reader 2:   they shall be destroyed forever.
Audience: But you, LORD, are most High for evermore.
Reader 1: O LORD, your enemies shall perish;
Reader 2:   all the workers of iniquity shall be scattered.
Reader 1: I shall be anointed with fresh oil.
Reader 2: My eye also shall see my desire on my enemies
Reader 1:   and my ears shall hear my desire
Reader 2:   of the wicked that rise up against me.

Choir:	The righteous shall flourish like the palm tree.
Audience:	They shall grow like a cedar in Lebanon.
Reader 2:	Those that are planted in the house of the LORD
Reader 1:	shall flourish in the courts of our God.
Reader 2:	They shall still bring forth fruit in old age.
Reader 1:	They shall be fat and flourishing
Reader 2:	showing that the LORD is upright.
Audience:	He is my rock,
Reader 2:	and there is no unrighteousness in him.
Reader 1:	This ends the reading.

A Mighty God
Adapted from Psalm 93
Readers 1,2

Introduction
Reader 1: Listen as we read Psalm 93
Reader 2:   extolling the virtues of our God.

Psalm 93
Reader 1: The LORD reigns,
Reader 2:   he is clothed with majesty.
Reader 1: The LORD is clothed with strength,
Reader 2:   wherewith he has clothed himself.
Reader 1: The world also is established
Reader 2:   that it cannot be moved.
Reader 1: Your throne is established of old.
Reader 2: You are from everlasting.
Reader 1: The floods have lifted up, O LORD,
Reader 2:   the floods have lifted up their voice,
Reader 1:   the floods lift up their waves.
Reader 2: The LORD on high is mightier
    than the noise of many waters,
Reader 1:   than the mighty waves of the sea.
Reader 2: Your testimonies are very sure.
Reader 1: Holiness becomes your house, O LORD, forever.
Reader 2: This ends the reading.

Call to Worship
Adapted from Psalm 95
Readers 1,2, Choir

Introduction

Reader 2: Our reading is a call to worship God

Reader 1:   not as the Israelites of old did,

Reader 2:   but in the joy of His salvation.

Reader 1: And now the reading of Psalm 95.

Psalm 95

Choir: O come, let us sing unto the LORD.

Reader 1: Let us make a joyful noise to the rock of our salvation.

Reader 2: Let us come before His presence with thanksgiving,

Reader 1:   and make a joyful noise to Him with psalms,

Choir: for the LORD is a great God

Reader 2:   and a great King above all gods.

Reader 1: In His hand are the deep places of the earth.

Reader 2: The strength of the hills is His.

Reader 1: The sea is His, and He made it

Reader 2:   and His hands formed the dry land.

Choir: O come, let us worship and bow down.

Reader 2: Let us kneel before the LORD our maker,

Reader 1:   for He is our God.

Choir: We are the people of His pasture,

Reader 2:   and the sheep of His hand.

Reader 1: Today, if you will hear His voice,

Reader 2:   harden not your heart, as in the provocation,

Reader 1:   and as in the day of temptation in the wilderness

Reader 2:   when your fathers tempted the Lord.

Choir: Forty years long I grieved with this generation.

Reader 1:   It is a people that do err in their hearts

Reader 2:   and they have not known my ways

Reader 1:   to whom I swear in my wrath

Reader 2:   that they should not enter into my rest.

Choir: But now, *let us* sing unto the LORD.

Reader 1:   *Let us* make a joyful noise to the rock of our salvation.

Reader 2:   This ends the reading.

Praise and Judgment

Adapted from Psalm 96

Reader 1,2, Choir

Introduction

Reader 1:   The first part of this reading

Reader 2:   is reminder that all are to praise God.

Reader 1:   The last part of this reading

Reader 2:   is a reminder that there will a judgment.

Reader 1:   Listen as Psalm 96 is read.

Psalm 96

Reader 1:   O sing to the LORD a new song.

Choir: Sing to the LORD, all the earth.

Reader 2:   Sing to the LORD, bless His name.

Reader 1:   Show forth His salvation from day to day.

Reader 2:   Declare His glory among the heathen,

Reader 1:   His wonders among all people

Choir: for the LORD is great

Reader 2:   and greatly to be praised.

Reader 1:   He is to be feared above all gods.

Reader 2:   All the gods of the nations are idols,

Choir: but the LORD made the heavens.

Reader 1:   Honor and majesty are before Him:

Reader 2:   strength and beauty are in His sanctuary.

Reader 1:   Give to the LORD,

Choir: give to the LORD glory and strength.

Reader 2:   Give to the LORD the glory due to His name,

Reader 1:   bring an offering and come into His courts.

Choir: O worship the LORD in the beauty of holiness,

Reader 2:   fear before Him, all the earth.

Reader 1:   Say among the heathen that the LORD reigns:

Reader 2:   the world also shall be established
            that it shall not be moved.

Reader 1:   He shall judge the people righteously.

Choir: Let the heavens rejoice

Reader 1:   and let the earth be glad.

Reader 2:   Let the sea roar, and the fullness thereof.

Choir: Let the field be joyful, all that is therein:

Reader 2:   then shall all the trees of the wood rejoice
            before the LORD:

Reader 1:   for He cometh to judge the earth.

Reader 2:   He shall judge the world with righteousness

Reader 1:   and the people with His truth.

Choir: O sing to the LORD a new song.

Reader 2:   Thanks be to God for these words.

Power and Protection
Adapted from Psalm 97
Reader 1,2, Audience, Choir

Introduction

Reader 1: Our reading recounts the power of God

Reader 2:   against which no force can prevail.

Reader 1: It is this power that cares for and protects His people.

Reader 2: Join with us in reading Psalm 97.

Psalm 97

Reader 1: The LORD reigns!

Audience: Let the earth rejoice.

Choir: Let the multitude of people be glad.

Reader 2: Clouds and darkness are round about Him,

Reader 1:   yet righteousness and judgment
are the corner stones of His throne.

Audience: A fire goes before Him,

Choir: and burns up His enemies round about.

Reader 2: His lightning lights up the world

Reader 1:   and all see and tremble.

Reader 2: The hills melt like wax at the presence of the LORD.

Reader 1: The heavens declare His righteousness

Reader 2:   and all the people see His glory.

Audience: All are confounded who serve graven images.

Choir: All are confused who boast themselves of idols.

Reader 1: Worship Him, all you idols.

Reader 2: Zion heard, and was glad

Reader 1:   and the daughters of Judah rejoiced

Reader 2:   because of your judgments, O LORD.

Audience: For you, LORD, are high above the earth.

Choir: You are exalted far above all gods.

Reader 1: You who love the LORD, hate evil.

Choir: He preserves the souls of His saints.

Reader 2:   He delivers them out of the hand of the wicked.

Reader 1:   Light is sown for the righteous

Reader 2:   and gladness for the upright in heart.

Audience: Rejoice in the LORD

Reader 1:   and give thanks at the remembrance of His holiness.

Reader 2:   Thanks be to God for these words.

Glory and Joy
Adapted from Psalm 98
Reader 1,2, Audience, Choir

Introduction
Reader 1: The glory of the Lord, our Redeemer,

Reader 2:   is well worded in the first part of this Psalm

Reader 1:   followed by the joy of salvation by our Redeemer.

Reader 2: Join us in reading from Psalm 98.

Psalm 98
Choir: O sing unto the LORD a new song.

Reader 1: He has done marvelous things.

Reader 2: His right hand, and His holy arm,
     has gotten him the victory.

Audience: The LORD has made known His salvation.

Reader 1: He has shown his righteousness to the heathen.

Audience: He has remembered His mercy

Choir: and His truth toward the house of Israel.

Reader 1: All the ends of the earth have seen the salvation
    of our God.

Audience: Make a joyful noise unto the LORD.

Reader 2: Make a loud noise, and rejoice, and sing praise.

Reader 1: Sing unto the LORD with the harp,

Choir: with the voice of a psalm.

Reader 1: With trumpets and sound of cornet

Audience: make a joyful noise before the LORD.

Reader 2: Let the sea roar

Reader 1:   and everything in it,

Reader 2:   and all who dwell therein.

Choir: Let the floods clap their hands.

Reader 1:   Let the hills be joyful together before the LORD;

Reader 2:   for He cometh to judge the earth with righteousness

Reader 1:   and the people with justice.

Choir: Thanks be to God for these words.

Traits of God's Government

Adapted from Psalm 99

Readers 1,2,3,4

Introduction

Reader 1: The reading details how God rules,

Reader 2:   how we are to respond to His rules.

Reader 1: Listen as we read Psalm 99.

Psalm 99

Reader 3: The LORD reigns

Reader 4:   so let the people tremble.

Reader 1: He sits between the cherubim.

Reader 2: The LORD is great in Zion

Reader 3:   and He is high above all the people.

Reader 1: Let them praise your great and terrible name,
    for it is holy.

Reader 3: The king's strength also loves judgment.

Reader 4: You establish equity.

Reader 2: You execute judgment and righteousness in Jacob.

Reader 1: Exalt the LORD our God

Reader 4:   and worship at his footstool for He is holy.

Reader 3: Moses and Aaron called on the LORD

Reader 2:   and He answered them in the cloudy pillar.

Reader 1: They kept His testimonies and the ordinances
    that He gave them.

Reader 3: You answered them, O LORD our God.

Reader 2: You were a God that forgave them,

Reader 4:   though you took vengeance of their deeds.

Reader 3: Exalt the LORD our God

Reader 1:   and worship at His holy hill;

Reader 2:   for the LORD our God is holy.

Reader 4: This ends the reading.

Invitation to Worship
Adapted from Psalm 100
Reader 1,2, Audience, Choir

Introduction

Reader 1: Long before we set aside one day a year in celebration of Thanksgiving,

Reader 2: David wrote from the depth of experiences with God

Reader 1: his reasons and our reasons to be thankful,

Reader 2: to be joyful.

Reader 1: Psalm 100 is both a testimony of what God has and is doing

Reader 2: and a prayer for His presence.

Reader 1: Let us read with the congregation and choir

Reader 2: David's timeless words of praise and thanksgiving.

Psalm 100

Choir: Shout joyfully to the Lord, everyone,

Reader 1: and serve the Lord with gladness and thanksgiving,

Reader 2: coming before Him with joyful singing.

Audience: Know that the Lord Himself is God.

Choir: Know that the Lord Himself has made us

Reader 1: and not we ourselves.

Audience: We are His people,

Reader 1: the work of His creation,

Reader 2: the sheep of His pasture.

Reader 1: Enter these doors, His doors, with thanksgiving,

Reader 2: and this sanctuary, His sanctuary, with praise.

Choir: Give thanks to Him!

Audience: Bless His name!

Reader 1: For the Lord is good,

Reader 2: and His faithfulness is to all generations.

Audience: His loving kindness is everlasting.

Reader 1:   Let us pray for His presence today
Reader 2:   to be enveloped in His holiness
Reader 1:   with a thankful heart and spirit.
   Choir: Amen and amen.

Who God Is

Adapted from Psalm 103
Reader 1,2, Audience, Choir

Introduction

Reader 1: This psalm calls for commitment.

Reader 2: It is a most superb psalm of praise.

Reader 1: It defines who God is by what He does.

Reader 2: The reading begins and ends with blessing to God.

Reader 1: Let us read together Psalm 103

Psalm 103

Reader 2: Bless the LORD, O my soul and all that is within me,

Reader 1: bless His holy name and forget not all His benefits:

Choir: who forgives all your sins,

Reader 1: who heals all your diseases,

Choir: who redeems your life from destruction,

Reader 2: who crowns you with loving
kindness and tender mercies,

Reader 1: who satisfies your mouth with good things,

Reader 2: so that your youth is renewed like the eagle's.

Reader 1: The LORD executes righteousness

Reader 2: and judgment for all that are oppressed.

Reader 1: He made known His ways unto Moses.

Reader 2: His acts to the children of Israel.

Audience: The LORD is merciful and gracious,

Choir: slow to anger and abundant in mercy.

Reader 1: However, He will not always rebuke,

Reader 2: neither will He keep His anger forever.

Reader 1: He has not rewarded us according to our sins.

Reader 2: For as the heaven is high above the earth,

Reader 1: so great is his mercy toward them that fear Him.

Audience: As far as the east is from the west,

Choir: so far has he removed our sins from us.

Reader 1: Like as a father pities his children,

Reader 2:   so the LORD pities them that fear Him.

Audience: For He knows our frame;

Choir: He remembers that we are dust.

Reader 1: As for us, our days are as grass,

Reader 2:   as a flower of the field.

Reader 1: The wind passes over it, and it is gone

Reader 2:   and the place thereof shall know it no more.

Reader 1: But the mercy of the LORD is
                 from everlasting to everlasting

Reader 2:   on them that fear Him

Reader 1:   and to such as keep His commandments to do them.

Reader 2: The LORD has prepared His throne in the heavens

Reader 1:   and His kingdom rules over all.

Reader 2: Bless the LORD, all you His angels,
                 which excel in strength,

Reader 1:   who do His commandments,
                 listening to the voice of His word.

Audience: Bless the LORD, all who do His pleasure.

Reader 2: Bless the LORD, O my soul and all that is within me,

Reader 1:   bless His holy name and forget not all His benefits.

Reader 2: Thanks be to God for these words.

God the Creator and Sustainer
Adapted from Psalm 104 (1st part)
Readers 1,2,3,4

Introduction

Reader 1: The author recounts metaphorically the creation
of the ocean and land

Reader 2: with a series of rhetorical questions

Reader 1: dealing with the majesty of God

Reader 2: in providing for all His created beings.

Reader 1: And now the reading from the first part of Psalm 104.

Psalm 104 (1st part)

Reader 1: Bless the LORD, O my soul.

Reader 2: You are very great.

Reader 3: You are clothed with honor and majesty.

Reader 4: Who covers you with light as with a garment?

Reader 3: Who stretches out the heavens like a curtain?

Reader 4: Who lays the beams of His chambers in the waters?

Reader 3: Who makes the clouds His chariot?

Reader 4: Who walks upon the wings of the wind?

Reader 3: Who makes His angels spirits?

Reader 4: Who makes His ministers a flaming fire?

Reader 3: Who laid the foundations of the earth,

Reader 4:   that it should not be removed forever?

All: The Lord, the Lord strong and mighty.

Reader 2: You covered it as with a garment.

Reader 1: The waters stood above the mountains;

Reader 2:   at your rebuke they fled.

Reader 1: At the voice of your thunder they passed away.

Reader 2: They go up by the mountains.

Reader 1: They go down by the valleys to the place
that you have founded for them.

Reader 4:   You have set a bound that they may not pass over

Reader 1:   so that they will not cover the earth again.

Reader 4:   He sends the springs into the valleys

Reader 3:   watering the hills from His chambers.

Reader 2:   They give drink to every beast of the field.

Reader 1:   By them shall the fowls of the heaven
                      have their habitation.

Reader 4:   The earth is satisfied with the fruit of your works.

Reader 3:   He causes the grass to grow for the cattle

Reader 2:   and herb for the service of man,

Reader 1:   that he may bring food out of the earth

Reader 3:   wine that makes glad the heart of man,

Reader 2:   oil to make his face to shine,

Reader 4:   and bread which strengthens man's heart.

Reader 1:   Bless the LORD, O my soul.

        All: You are very great!

Reader 1:   This ends the reading.

Protection and Praises
Adapted from Psalm 104 (2nd part)
Readers 1,2,3,4

Introduction

Reader 1: This passage from Psalms is filled with metaphors

Reader 2:   of God's absolute control over His creation.

Reader 1: The passage ends with praises to God.

Reader 2: Listen as the second part of Psalm 104 is now read.

Psalm 104 (2nd part)

Reader 3: Bless the LORD, O my soul.

Reader 4:   because you are very great

Reader 1:   you are clothed with honor and majesty.

Reader 2: The cedars of Lebanon which He has planted
    are full of sap

Reader 3:   where the birds make their nests,

Reader 4:   as for the stork, the fir trees are her house,

Reader 1:   whereas the high hills are a refuge for the wild goats.

Reader 3: He appointed the moon for seasons.

Reader 4: The sun knows his going down.

Reader 2: You make darkness, and it is night

Reader 1:   wherein all the beasts of the forest do creep forth.

Reader 4: The young lions roar after their prey

Reader 3:   and seek their meat from God.

Reader 2: As the sun rises they gather themselves together

Reader 1:   and lie down in their dens;

Reader 2:   however, man goes to his work in the morning

Reader 4:   and to his labor until the evening.

Reader 2: O LORD, how manifold are your works!

Reader 3: In wisdom you have made them all.

Reader 1: The earth is full of your riches.

Reader 4:   So is this great and wide sea,

Reader 1:   wherein are things creeping innumerable,

Reader 3:   both small and great beasts including the leviathan.

Reader 2:   These wait all upon you; that you may give them
their meat in due season.

Reader 1:   When you open your hand they are filled with good.

Reader 4:   When you hide your face, they are troubled.

Reader 2:   When you take away their breath they die
and return to their dust.

Reader 1:   When you send forth your spirit they are created

Reader 3:   and the face of the earth is renewed.

Reader 2:   The glory of the LORD shall endure forever.

Reader 4:   The LORD shall rejoice in his works,

Reader 1:   as He looks on the earth and it trembles.

Reader 3:   He touches the hills and they smoke.

Reader 1:   I will sing to the LORD as long as I live.

Reader 2:   I will sing praise to my God while I have my being.

Reader 3:   My meditation of Him shall be sweet.

Reader 4:   I will be glad in the LORD.

Reader 2:   Let the sinners be consumed out of the earth

Reader 1:   and let the wicked be no more.

Reader 3:   Bless the LORD, O my soul.

Reader 4:   You are very great

Reader 1:   because you are clothed with honor and majesty.

Reader 2:   This ends the reading

Reader 3:   and thanks be to God for this word.

Praise And Deliverance
Adapted from Psalm 105
Reader 1,2, Audience, Choir

Introduction

Reader 1: The first part of this reading is a call to praise.

Reader 2: The second part of this reading describes
God's contact with Israel.

Reader 1: Finally the reading recounts the liberation from Egypt.

Reader 2: Join with us in reading from Psalm 105.

Psalm 105

Reader 1: O give thanks to the LORD, call on His name

Reader 2:   and make known His deeds among the people.

Choir: Sing to Him, talk of all His wondrous works.

Audience: Glory in His holy name.

Reader 1: Seek the LORD and His strength

Reader 2:   remembering His marvelous works.

Audience: He is the LORD our God.

Choir: He has remembered His covenant forever,

Reader 1:   that He made with Abraham, Isaac, and Jacob.

Reader 2: Saying to them I will give you the land of Canaan

Reader 1:   when they were but few and strangers in it.

Reader 2: When they went from one nation to another,

Choir: God said, touch not my anointed

Reader 1:   and do my prophets no harm.

Reader 2: Moreover He called for a famine on the land,

Reader 1:   but He sent a man before them, even Joseph,

Reader 2:   who was sold for a servant.

Reader 1: Whose feet they hurt with fetters; he was laid in iron

Reader 2:   until the king sent and loosed him

Reader 1:   and let him go free.

Reader 2: He made him lord and ruler of all his substance,

Reader 1:	to bind his princes at his pleasure.
Audience:	God increased his people greatly
Choir:	and made them stronger than their enemies.
Reader 2:	He turned the Egyptian's heart to hate his people.
Reader 1:	He sent Moses and Aaron, whom He had chosen,
Audience:	to show His signs among them.
Choir:	He sent darkness, and made it dark.
Reader 1:	He turned their waters into blood, and slew their fish.
Audience:	He brought forth frogs in abundance
Choir:	even in the chambers of their kings.
Reader 2:	He spoke and there came flies and lice.
Reader 1:	He gave them hail for rain.
Reader 2:	He spoke and the locusts and caterpillars came without number
Reader 1:	and devoured the fruit of their ground.
Reader 2:	He smote also all the firstborn in their land.
Reader 1:	He brought them forth with silver and gold
Reader 2:	and there was not one sick person among them.
Audience:	Egypt was glad when they departed
Reader 1:	for the fear of them fell on them.
Reader 2:	He spread a cloud for a covering
Reader 1:	and fire to give light in the night.
Reader 2:	The people asked and He brought quails
Reader 1:	and satisfied them with the bread of heaven.
Choir:	He opened the rock,
Audience:	and the waters gushed out.
Reader 2:	For He remembered His holy promise to Abraham.
Reader 1:	He brought forth his people with joy and gladness.
Reader 2:	He gave them the lands of the heathen
Reader 1:	that they might observe and keep His laws.
Audience:	Praise ye the LORD.
Reader 2:	This ends the reading.

Prophecy of the Messiah
Adapted from Psalm 110
Reader 1,2, Audience

Introduction

Reader 1:   Jesus quoted from this Psalm written by David

Reader 2:   to confound the religious leaders.

Reader 1:   It is a Psalm that is prophetic in nature

Reader 2:   of the life of God's son

Reader 1:   and the ultimate triumph of God's kingdom.

Reader 2:   Let us join together in the reading of Psalm 110.

Psalm 110

Reader 1:   The LORD said unto my Lord,

Audience: Sit at my right hand,

Reader 2:   until I make your enemies my footstool.

Reader 1:   The LORD shall send the rod of your
    strength out of Zion, declaring,

Audience: Rule in the midst of your enemies.

Reader 2:   Your people shall be willing in the day of your power,

Reader 1:   in the beauties of holiness from the womb
    of the morning

Reader 2:   you have the dew of your youth.

Reader 1:   The LORD has sworn,

Audience: and will not repent,

Reader 2:   Your are a priest forever after the order
    of Melchizedek.

Audience: The Lord at your right hand

Reader 1:   shall strike through kings in the day of is wrath.

Reader 2:   He shall judge among the heathen.

Reader 1:   He shall fill the places with the dead bodies.

Reader 2: He shall wound the heads over many countries.
Reader 1: He shall drink of the brook along the way;
Reader 2:   therefore, shall He lift His head high.
Reader 1: This ends the reading.

Praise the Lord
Adapted from Psalm 111
Readers 1,2, Audience

Introduction

Reader 1:   This Psalm, penned by David,

Reader 2:   is well adapted for introducing a worship service.

Reader 1:   It relates the attributes of God

Reader 2:   for which we need to praise Him.

Reader 1:   Join with us in reading Psalm 111.

Psalm 111

Reader 1:   Praise the LORD.

Reader 2:   I will praise the LORD with my whole heart,

Reader 1:   in the midst of the upright.

Audience: The Lord is great.

Reader 1:   His work is honorable and glorious

Reader 2:   and His righteousness endures forever.

Reader 1:   He has made His wonderful works to be remembered.

Audience: The LORD is gracious and full of compassion.

Reader 2:   He has given food to them that fear Him

Reader 1:   and is ever mindful of His promise.

Reader 2:   He has showed his people the power of His works,

Reader 1:   that He may give them the heritage of the heathen.

Reader 2:   The works of His hands are truth and judgment.

Audience: All His commandments are sure.

Reader 1:   They stand fast forever and ever

Reader 2:   and are done in truth and uprightness.

Reader 1:   He sent redemption to His people.

Reader 2:   He has commanded His promise forever;

Audience: holy and reverend is His name!

Reader 1:   The fear of the LORD is the beginning of wisdom.

Reader 2:   They that do His commandments
Reader 1:   have good understanding.
Audience: Praise the LORD.
Reader 2:   I will praise the LORD with my whole heart.
Reader 1:   This ends the reading.

Praise of the Righteous
Adapted from Psalm 112
Readers 1,2, Choir

Introduction
Reader 1: In this reading we are exhorted to praise the Lord
Reader 2:   because of the many benefits He has bestowed on us.
Reader 1: Let us read together Psalm 112.

Psalm 112
Reader 1: Praise ye the LORD.
Choir: Blessed are those that fear the LORD,
Reader 2:   who delight greatly in His commandments.
Choir: Their descendants shall be great throughout earth
Reader 1:   and their children who do right shall be blessed.
Reader 2: Wealth and riches shall be in their house
Reader 1:   and their righteousness shall endure forever.
Reader 2: They are a light in the darkness because
Reader 1:   they are gracious, full of compassion, and righteous.
Choir: Good people show favor and lend.
Reader 2: They will guide their affairs with discretion.
Choir: Surely they shall not be moved forever.
Reader 1: The righteous shall be in everlasting remembrance.
Reader 2: They shall not be afraid of evil news because
Reader 1:   their hearts are unchanged in trusting in the LORD.
Reader 2: Their hearts are established, they shall not be afraid,
Reader 1:   until they see their desire upon their enemies.
Reader 2: Since they have given to the poor
Choir: their righteousness endures forever.
Reader 1: The wicked shall see it and are grieved,
Reader 2:   gnashing their teeth, and fading away
Reader 1: The wants of the wicked come to nothing.
Reader 2: This ends the reading.

Praise for He Cares for the Poor
Adapted from Psalm 113
Readers 1,2, Choir

Introduction

Reader 1: Psalm 113 is a typical Psalm of praise to God.

Reader 2: Praise is particularly given due to His treatment of the poor.

Reader 1: This is a demonstration of how we should treat the less fortunate.

Reader 2: Let us read together Psalm 113.

Psalm 113

Choir: Praise ye the LORD.

Reader 1: Praise, O ye servants of the LORD.

Choir: Praise the name of the LORD.

Reader 2: Blessed be the name of the LORD for evermore.

Reader 1: From the rising of the sun

Reader 2: to the going down of the same

Choir: the LORD's name is to be praised.

Reader 1: The LORD is high above all nations

Reader 2: and His glory above the heavens.

Choir: Who is like the LORD our God?

Reader 1: Who humbles Himself

Reader 2: to see the things in heaven and earth?

Reader 1: He raises up the poor out of the dust,

Reader 2: and lifts the needy out of the dunghill,

Reader 1: that He may set them with princes,

Reader 2: even with the princes of His people.

Reader 1: He makes the barren woman to keep house

Reader 2: and to be a joyful mother of children.

Choir: Praise ye the LORD.

Reader 2: This ends the reading.

Our God Is Alive
Adapted from Psalm 115
Readers 1,2,3,4

Introduction

Reader 1: The writer of the reading gives

Reader 2: a list of powerful arguments against the value

Reader 1: of idols those men have made.

Reader 2: The reading ends with the assurance that God is alive.

Reader 1: Here is the reading taken from Psalm 115.

Psalm 115

Reader 3: Oh Lord, we give you glory,

Reader 4: for your mercy and for your truth's sake.

Reader 3: The heathen may say, Where is your God now?

Reader 4: Our God is in the heavens

Reader 3: and He has done whatever he pleases.

Reader 4: Their idols are silver and gold,

Reader 3: the work of men's hands.

Reader 1: They have mouths,

Reader 2: but they speak not.

Reader 1: Eyes they have,

Reader 2: but they see not.

Reader 1: They have ears,

Reader 2: but they hear not.

Reader 1: Noses they have,

Reader 2: but they smell not.

Reader 1: They have hands,

Reader 2: but they handle not.

Reader 1: Feet they have,

Reader 2: but they walk not.

Reader 1: Neither speaks they through their throat.

Reader 2:   They who make them are like unto them
Reader 1:   so is every one that trusts in them.
Reader 3:   Israel, trust in the LORD,
Reader 4:   He is your help and your shield.
Reader 3:   The LORD has been mindful of us.
Reader 4:   He will bless them that fear the LORD,
Reader 3:   both small and great.
Reader 4:   The LORD shall increase you more and more,
Reader 3:   you and your children.
Reader 4:   You are blessed of the LORD
                who made heaven and earth.
Reader 3:   The heaven, even the heavens, are the LORD's,
Reader 4:   but the earth has He given to the children of men.
Reader 3:   The dead praise not the LORD,
Reader 4:   neither any that go down into silence.
Reader 3:   But we will bless the LORD
Reader 4:   from this time forth and for evermore.
Reader 3:   Praise the LORD.

David's Testimony
Adapted from Psalm 116
Readers 1,2,3

Introduction
Reader 3:   Listen as David recounts his reasons
Reader 2:   for calling on the name of the Lord
Reader 3:   and committing himself to be a servant of God.
Reader 2:   And now the reading from Psalm 116.

Psalm 116
Reader 1:   I love the LORD,
Reader 2:   because He heard his supplications,
Reader 3:   because He inclined his ear to him;
Reader 1:   therefore, I will call unto God during my whole life.
Reader 2:   The sorrows of death compassed him
Reader 3:   and the pains of hell got hold on him.
Reader 1:   I found trouble and sorrow;
Reader 2:   then he called upon the name of the LORD.
Reader 1:   I beseech you, deliver my soul.
Reader 3:   Gracious and merciful is the LORD.
Reader 1:   I was brought low and He helped me.
Reader 2:   The LORD had dealt bountifully with him.
Reader 3:   He delivered his soul from death,
Reader 2:   his eyes from tears,
Reader 3:   and his feet from falling.
Reader 1:   I will walk before the LORD in the land of the living.
Reader 3:   What should he render unto the LORD
Reader 2:   for all his benefits toward him?
Reader 1:   I will take the cup of salvation
Reader 3:   and he called on the name of the LORD.
Reader 1:   I will pay my vows to the LORD in the presence
                of all His people.

Reader 3:   Precious in the sight of the LORD is the death
　　　　　　　　of his saints.
Reader 1:   O LORD, truly I am your servant.
Reader 2:   He then offered to God the sacrifice of thanksgiving
Reader 3:   and he called on the Lord's name
Reader 2:   in the courts of the LORD's house.
Reader 1:   I will praise the LORD.
Reader 2:   This ends the reading.

The Kingdom of Trust

Adapted from Psalm 118
Readers 1,2,3, Audience

Introduction

Reader 3: In the first part of the reading David

Reader 2:   affirms that it is good to trust in the Lord.

Reader 3: In the second part of the reading David anticipates

Reader 2:   and celebrates the coming of God's kingdom.

Reader 3: Join with us in this reading from Psalm 118.

Psalm 118

Reader 1: O give thanks unto the LORD,

Audience: for He is good,

Reader 3:   because His mercy endures forever.

Reader 1: Let Israel now say,

Audience: that His mercy endures forever.

Reader 1: Let them know that fear the LORD say,

Audience: that His mercy endures forever.

Reader 1: I called upon the LORD in distress,

Reader 3:   the LORD answered me.

Reader 2: The LORD is on my side.

Reader 1: I will not fear, what can man do to me?

Audience: It is better to trust in the LORD

Reader 1:   than to put confidence in man.

Audience: It is better to trust in the LORD

Reader 3:   than to put confidence in princes.

Reader 2: The nations surrounded me,

Reader 3:   but in the name of the LORD will I destroy them.

Reader 2: They surrounded me about like bees,

Reader 1:   for in the name of the LORD I will destroy them.

Audience: The LORD is my strength and song

Reader 1:   and is become my salvation.

Reader 2:   The voice of rejoicing and salvation

Reader 3:   is in the tabernacles of the righteous,

Reader 2:   I shall not die, but live

Reader 1:   and declare the works of the LORD.

Reader 2:   The LORD has chastened me sorely,

Reader 3:   but He has not given me over to die.

Reader 1:   Open the gates of righteousness;

Audience: I will go into them,

Reader 1:   and I will praise the LORD.

Reader 2:   I will praise you,

Reader 3:   for you have heard me

Reader 2:   and is become my salvation.

Reader 3:   The stone which the builders refused

Reader 1:   is become the head stone of the corner.

Audience: This is the LORD's doing, it is marvelous.

Reader 1:   This is the day that the LORD has made,

Audience: we will rejoice and be glad in it.

Reader 1:   O LORD, I beseech you, send success.

Audience: Blessed is he that comes in the name of the LORD.

Reader 1:   God is the LORD,
                    who has showed us the lighted pathway.

Reader 3:   You are my God, I will praise you.

Reader 1:   You are my God, I will exalt you.

Audience: O give thanks unto the LORD,

Reader 1:   for He is good,

Reader 3:   for His mercy endures forever.

Reader 2:   Thanks be to God for these words.

A Believer's Experience
Adapted from Psalm 119:1-8
Readers 1,2, Audience

Introduction
Reader 1:   Our reading lists the conditions for being blessed.

Reader 2:   Let us read together Psalm 119:1-8

Psalm 119:1-8
Reader 1:   Blessed are they:

Reader 2:   who are undefiled,

Audience: who walk in the law of the LORD.

Reader 1:   Blessed are they:

Reader 2:   who keep His testimonies,

Audience: who seek Him with the whole heart,

Reader 1:   who do no iniquity,

Audience: who walk in His ways.

Reader 1:   Blessed are they:

Reader 2:   who keep His precepts diligently,
                 who keep His statutes,

Audience: who will not be ashamed,

Reader 2:   when we have respected all His commandments.

Audience: Praise Him with all our hearts,

Reader 1:   since we learned His righteous judgments.

Reader 2:   We will keep His statutes.

Audience: O Lord do not forsake us.

Young People Heed the Scriptures
Adapted from Psalm 119:9-16
Readers 1,2, Choir

Introduction

Reader 1:   While this reading is addressed to young people

Reader 2:   it applies to all

Reader 1:   who would lead a Godly life.

Reader 2:   Listen to the secrets of a spirit-filled existence

Reader 1:   as we read together Psalm 119:9-16.

Psalm 119:9-16

Reader 2:   How will young persons cleanse their way?

Choir: By heeding the instruction in your word.

Reader 1:   With my whole being have I sought you.

Reader 2:   O let me not stray from your commandments.

Choir: Your word have I hid in mine heart,

Reader 2:   that I might not sin against you.

Reader 1:   Blessed are you, O LORD,

Reader 2:   teach me your statutes.

Reader 1:   With my lips have I declared

Reader 2:   all the judgments of your mouth.

Reader 1:   I have rejoiced in the way of your advice,

Reader 2:   as much as riches.

Choir: I will meditate in your precepts,

Reader 2:   and have respect unto your ways.

Reader 1:   I will delight myself in your statutes.

Choir: I will not forget your word.

Reader 2:   This ends the reading.

I Am a Stranger in the Earth

Adapted from Psalm 119:17-24
Readers 1,2, Audience

Introduction

Reader 1: In our short reading for today in Psalm 119:17-24

Reader 2: the writer prays for new insights

Reader 1: into the laws of the Lord.

Reader 2: The reading ends taking pleasure
in the Lord's laws and advice.

Psalm 119:17-24

Reader 1: Deal kindly with your servant

Audience: Open my eyes,

Reader 1: that I may live,

Reader 2: that I may keep your word,

Reader 1: that I may behold wondrous things out of your law.

Audience: I am a stranger in the earth,

Reader 1: hide not your commandments from me.

Reader 2: At all times my whole being longs for your laws.

Reader 1: You rebuke and curse the arrogant,

Reader 2: which do err from your commandments.

Audience: Remove from me reproach and contempt

Reader 2: for I have kept your laws.

Reader 1: Princes sit and speak against me:

Reader 2: but your servant did think thoughts of you.

Reader 1: Your laws and advice

Audience: are my delight and my counselors.

Reader 2: This ends the reading.

Walking in the Light

Adapted from Psalm 119:25-32

Readers 1,2, Audience

Introduction

Reader 1: The reading is both a prayer for a better understanding

Reader 2:   of the ways of the Lord

Reader 1:   and an appeal for grace.

Reader 2: Finally it acknowledges

Reader 1:   that freedom comes through obedience.

Reader 2: Join with us in reading from Psalm 119:25-32.

Psalm 119:25-32

Reader 1: My whole being is laid low in the ground.

Audience: Make me alive according to your word.

Reader 1: I have told my ways to you,

Reader 2:   and you heard me, now teach me your ways.

Audience: O Lord, help me to understand

Reader 2:   the teachings of your precepts,

Reader 1:   so shall I talk of your wondrous works.

Reader 2: My whole being is very weary,

Reader 1:   so strengthen me according to your word.

Reader 2: Keep me from being deceitful.

Audience: Grant me grace within your law.

Reader 2: I have chosen the way of truth.

Reader 1: Your judgments are ever before me.

Reader 2: I have stuck to your teachings.

Audience: O Lord, put me not to shame.

Reader 2: I will walk in the ways of your commandments,

Audience: then I shall be free, free at last.

Reader 1: This ends the reading.

Teach Me Lord
Adapted from Psalm 119:33-40
Readers 1,2, Audience

Introduction

Reader 1:   The reading is a prayer
Reader 2:   that could well be our own.
Reader 1:   It is a prayer for understanding
Reader 2:   and the desire to have a changed life.
Reader 1:   Let us read together Psalm 119:33-40.

Psalm 119:33-40

Reader 1:   Teach me, O LORD, the way of your statutes
Reader 2:   and I shall keep it all the days of my life.
Audience: Give me understanding,
Reader 2:   and I shall keep your law.
Audience: I shall keep it with my whole being.
Reader 2:   Lead me down the path of your commandments
Reader 1:   for therein do I delight.
Reader 2:   Turn my heart toward your testimonies:
Reader 1:   not to be covetous,
Reader 2:   not to be deceitful.
Audience: Hasten to change my life
Reader 2:   by establishing your word in your servant,
Reader 1:   who is devoted to you.
Reader 2:   Take away my shame,
Reader 1:   for your judgments are good.
Reader 2:   I have longed after your precepts.
Audience: Make me alive in your righteousness.
Reader 1:   Amen. This ends the reading.

Walking, Talking, Living for God
Adapted from Psalm 119:41-48
Readers 1,2

Introduction

Reader 1: The author of our reading today

Reader 2:   takes special note of the value of knowing

Reader 1:   and following the Lord's commandments.

Reader 2: Listen to these words from Psalm 119:41-48.

Psalm 119:41-48

Reader 1: O Lord, let your mercies come to me

Reader 2:   and your salvation,

Reader 1:   all according to your word.

Reader 2: Now I have the answer to him that taunts me.

Reader 1: It is your word!

Reader 2: Take not the word of truth utterly out of my mouth.

Reader 1: I have hoped in your judgments.

Reader 2: I keep your law continually forever and ever.

Reader 1: I will walk at liberty,

Reader 2:   for I seek your precepts.

Reader 1: I will speak of your testimonies before kings

Reader 2:   and will not be ashamed.

Reader 1: I will delight myself in your commandments

Reader 2:   which I have loved.

Reader 1: My hands will I lift up to your commandments

Reader 2:   which I have loved,

Reader 1:   and I will meditate in your statutes.

Reader 2: Thanks be to God for these words.

Making God's Promises Your Life.
Adapted from Psalm 119:49-56
Readers 1,2

Introduction

Reader 1: Today's reading from the book of Psalm 119:49-56

Reader 2:   is a prayer that recounts the comfort

Reader 1:   that God supplies in the face of wickedness.

Reader 2: The author reaffirms his practice

Reader 1:   of obeying the commandments of the Lord.

Reader 2: And now the prayer.

Psalm 119:49-56

Reader 1: Remember the word to your servant,

Reader 2:   it has caused me to hope.

Reader 1: This is my comfort in my affliction

Reader 2:   for your word has given me new life.

Reader 1: The arrogant taunt me greatly in derision,

Reader 2:   yet I still revere your law.

Reader 1: O Lord, I remembered your judgments of the past

Reader 2:   and have comforted myself.

Reader 1: I am appalled because of the wicked

Reader 2:   who have forsaken your law.

Reader 1: Your statutes have been my song
        in the house of my pilgrimage.

Reader 2: O Lord, I have remembered your name,

Reader 1:   day and night, I have kept your law.

Reader 2: It has been my custom

Reader 1:   to keep your precepts.

Reader 2: This ends the reading.

My Thoughts Are Thoughts of God

Adapted from Psalm 119:57-64

Readers 1,2

Introduction

Reader 1:   This short Psalm shows

Reader 2:   the commitment of the Psalmist

Reader 1:   to God in all ways of his life.

Reader 2:   Finally he declares the Lord is full of mercy.

Reader 1:   And now Psalm 119:57-44.

Psalm 119:57-44

Reader 1:   I promise that I will keep your words,

Reader 2:   you are my portion, O LORD.

Reader 1:   I entreat your favor with my whole being.

Reader 2:   Be merciful to me according to your word.

Reader 1:   I have thought on my life

Reader 2:   and turned my feet to your testimonies.

Reader 1:   I have made haste and did not delay

Reader 2:   to keep your commandments.

Reader 1:   The hordes of the wicked have robbed me,

Reader 2:   but I have not forgotten your law.

Reader 1:   Even at midnight I rise to give you thanks

Reader 2:   because of your righteous judgments.

Reader 1:   I am a companion and a friend of all who fear you

Reader 2:   and of them that keep your precepts.

Reader 1:   The world, O Lord, is full of your mercy.

Reader 2:   Teach me to obey your statutes.

Reader 1:   This ends the reading.

His Laws Are Desirable
Adapted from Psalm 119:65-72
Readers 1,2

Introduction

Reader 1: Throughout his life the Psalmist
Reader 2:   has lived a God-fearing life:
Reader 1:   in spite of the lies of the wicked,
Reader 2:   in spite of affliction,
Reader 1:   in recognition of the value of God's laws.
Reader 2: And now Psalm 119:65-72.

Psalm 119:65-72.

Reader 1: You have dealt well with your servant
Reader 2:   according to your word.
Reader 1: I have believed your commandments.
Reader 2: They have taught me good judgment and knowledge.
Reader 1: Before I was afflicted I went astray,
Reader 2:   but now I obey your word.
Reader 1: O Lord, you are good,
Reader 2:   and do what is good.
Reader 1: Teach me to do good.
Reader 2: The arrogant have invented lies against me:
Reader 1:   but I will keep your precepts with my whole being.
Reader 2: Their beings are as useless fat,
Reader 1:   but I delight in your law.
Reader 2: It is good that I have been afflicted.
Reader 1: In this affliction I have learned of your ways.
Reader 2: The laws from your mouth are better
Reader 1:   to me than thousands of pieces of gold and silver.
Reader 2: This ends the reading.

Pleas for Mercy

Adapted from Psalm 119:73-80

Readers 1,2, Audience

Introduction

Reader 1: The Psalmist acknowledges his debt to the Lord

Reader 2: for the Lord's kindness and mercy.

Reader 1: As is so familiar in the Psalms

Reader 2: the author is critical of those who deal
wickedly with him.

Reader 1: Listen to the pleas for mercy

Reader 2: as we read together Psalm 119:73-80.

Psalm 119:73-80

Reader 1: Your hands have

Reader 2: made me and fashioned me.

Audience: Give me understanding,

Reader 1: that I may learn your commandments.

Reader 2: They that fear you will be glad when they see me:

Reader 1: because I have hoped in your word.

Audience: Lord, your judgments are right

Reader 1: and in faithfulness you have afflicted me.

Reader 2: Let your merciful kindness be my comfort

Reader 1: as you have promised to your servant.

Audience: Let your tender mercies come to me

Reader 1: that I may live:

Reader 2: for your law is my delight.

Reader 1: Let the arrogant be ashamed,

Reader 2: for they dealt perversely with me
without a cause.

Audience: But I will meditate in your precepts.

Reader 2: Let those that fear you turn to me
Reader 1:   because I have known your testimonies.
Reader 2: Let my heart be sound in your statutes
Reader 1:   that I be not ashamed.
Reader 2: Amen.

Deliverance from His Sins
Adapted from Psalm 119:81-88
Readers 1,2

Introduction

Reader 1: In our reading for today
Reader 2:   the Psalmist complains to God
Reader 1:   concerning those who would destroy him.
Reader 2: So he wonders, when will justice be given?
Reader 1: Then a final plea to be made alive!
Reader 2: And now the reading from Psalm 119:81-88.

Ps 119:81-88

Reader 1: My soul faints with longing for your salvation
Reader 2:   but I hope in your word.
Reader 1: My eyes fail, looking for your promise.
Reader 2: When will you comfort me?
Reader 1: Though I am like a bottle in the smoke,
Reader 2:   yet I do not forget your statutes.
Reader 1: How many days must your servant wait?
Reader 2: When will you execute judgment
Reader 1:   on them that persecute me?
Reader 2: The arrogant dig pitfalls for me
Reader 1:   which is contrary to your law.
Reader 2: All your commandments are faithful.
Reader 1: Help me! Men persecute me wrongfully.
Reader 2: They had almost consumed my entire being,
Reader 1:   but I forsook not your precepts.
Reader 2: Make me alive with your loving kindness,
Reader 1:   so shall I keep the testimony of your mouth.
Reader 2: Thanks be to God for these words.

Law Is Settled in Heaven
Adapted from Psalm 119:89-93
Readers 1,2

Introduction
Reader 1: The reading extols the virtues
Reader 2:   of a God who is faithful.
Reader 1: This is followed with a commitment
Reader 2:   to never forget God's laws.
Reader 1: Listen as we read from Psalm 119:89-93.

Psalm 119:89-93
Reader 1: Forever, O Lord,
Reader 2:   your word is settled in heaven.
Reader 1: Your faithfulness is to all generations.
Reader 2: You have established the earth
Reader 1:   and made it secure.
Reader 2: The world continues this day
Reader 1:   according to your laws.
Reader 2: Unless I had obeyed your law with joy,
Reader 1:   I would have perished in my affliction.
Reader 2: I will never forget your precepts,
Reader 1:   for with them you have made me alive.
Reader 2: I am yours, save me,
Reader 1:   for I have sought your precepts.
Reader 2: Thanks be to God for these words.

Benefits of the Law of God
Adapted from Psalm 119:95-104
Reader 1,2, Audience

Introduction
Reader 1: The basis for this reading
Reader 2:   is based on the writer's thinking
Reader 1:   that the wicked wait to destroy him.
Reader 2: He finds refuge and wisdom in the commandments
Reader 1:   and the words of God.
Reader 2: Join us in reading from Psalm 119:95-104.

Psalm 119:95-104
Reader 1: The wicked have waited to destroy me,
Reader 2:   but I will consider your testimonies.
Reader 1: I have seen an end of all perfection,
Reader 2:   but your commandments
Reader 1:   are from everlasting to everlasting.
Audience: O, how I love your law!
Reader 1: It is my meditation all day.
Reader 2: Your commandments have made me
   wiser than my enemies,
Audience: because they are ever with me.
Reader 1: I have more understanding than all my teachers
Audience: because I meditate on your laws.
Reader 2: I understand more than the ancients
Audience: because I keep your precepts.
Reader 2: I have refrained my feet from every evil way
Audience: because I keep your word.
Reader 2: I have not departed from your judgments
Audience: because you have taught me.
Reader 2: How sweet are your words to my taste
Reader 1:   yea, sweeter than honey to my mouth!

Reader 2:   I hate every false way

Audience: because through your precepts I get understanding.

Reader 1:   This ends the reading.

God's Directions
Adapted from Psalm 119:105-112
Readers 1,2, Choir

Introduction

Reader 1: The first two lines of this reading

Reader 2: are perhaps some of the best known scripture

Reader 1: in all of the Psalms.

Reader 2: The writer is always aware the wicked

Reader 1: are about to destroy him,

Reader 2: in spite of his dedication to precepts of God.

Reader 1: And now the reading from Psalm 119:105-112.

Psalm 119:105-112

Choir: Your word is a lamp to my feet

Reader 2: and a light to my path.

Reader 1: I have sworn and I will perform it,

Reader 2: that I will keep your righteous judgments.

Reader 1: I am afflicted very much.

Choir: Make me alive, O Lord,

Reader 1: according to your word.

Reader 2: Accept, I plead with you,

Reader 1: the freewill offerings of my mouth

Reader 2: and teach me your judgments.

Choir: My life is continually in my hand

Reader 2: yet I do not forget your law.

Reader 1: The wicked have set a trap for me

Reader 2: yet I erred not from your precepts.

Reader 1: Your testimonies have I taken as an heritage forever,

Choir: for they are the rejoicing of my heart.

Reader 1: I have dedicated my life to perform your statutes,

Reader 2: even to the end.

Fear of Judgment
Adapted from Psalm 119:113-119
Readers 1,2

Introduction

Reader 1: The Psalmist places himself on the side of God,

Reader 2:   saying that keeping the commandments

Reader 1:   is his only safe place to be.

Reader 2: Yet he ultimately fears the impending judgment
of the Lord.

Reader 1: And now the reading from Psalm 119:113-119.

Psalm 119:113-119

Reader 1: I hate vain thoughts

Reader 2:   but your law do I love.

Reader 1: You are my hiding place:

Reader 2:   my shield,

Reader 1:   my hope.

Reader 2: Depart from me,

Reader 1:   you that do evil.

Reader 2: I will keep the commandments of my God.

Reader 1: Sustain me according to your word that I may live

Reader 2:   and not be ashamed of my hope.

Reader 1: Hold you me up

Reader 2:   and I shall be safe.

Reader 1: I will have respect to your statutes
and laws continually.

Reader 2: You have trodden down all those that err
from your statutes

Reader 1:   because their deceit is falsehood!

Reader 2: You put away all the wicked of the world like dross,

Reader 1:   therefore I love your testimonies.

Reader 2:   My whole body trembles for fear of you
Reader 1:   because I am afraid of your judgments.
Reader 2:   This ends the reading.

Love of the Law
Adapted from Psalm 119:121-128
Readers 1,2, Choir

Introduction
Reader 1: The Psalmist contrasts his relationship to God
Reader 2:   with his enemies.
Reader 1: Listen as the author expresses his love
Reader 2:   and adherence to the commandments of God.
Reader 1: Now hear Psalm 119:121-128.

Psalm 119:121-128
Reader 1: I have obeyed what is right,
Reader 2:   so do not leave me to my oppressors.
Reader 1: Protect your servant for good.
Reader 2: Don't let the arrogant oppress me.
Choir: I looked for your salvation
Reader 2:   but my eyes failed to see it.
Choir: I will look for the word of your righteousness.
Reader 2: Deal with your servant according to your mercy
Reader 1:   and teach me your statutes.
Choir: I am your servant,
Reader 1:   give me understanding,
Reader 2:   that I may know your testimonies.
Choir: It is time for you, Lord, to work
Reader 2:   because they have made void your law.
Reader 1: Therefore I love your commandments above gold
Reader 2:   yea, above fine gold.
Choir: I esteem all your precepts to be right
Reader 2:   and I hate every false way.
Reader 1: Thanks be to God for these words.

Triumph of God's Love
Adapted from Psalm 119:129-136
Readers 1,2

Introduction
Reader 1:   This prayer is an expression of gratitude

Reader 2:   and a petition for the Lord's guidance.

Reader 1:   It ends with a sad reflection

Reader 2:   on those who do not keep God's commandments.

Reader 1:   Now the reading from Psalm 119:129-136.

Psalm 119:129-136
Reader 1:   Your testimonies are wonderful;

Reader 2:   therefore, my soul shall keep them.

Reader 1:   The entrance of your words enlightens minds

Reader 2:   and it gives understanding to the simple.

Reader 1:   I opened my mouth, and breathed heavily.

Reader 2:   I longed for your commandments.

Reader 1:   Look on me,

Reader 2:   be merciful to me

Reader 1:   as one who loves your name.

Reader 2:   Direct my steps from your word

Reader 1:   and let not any evil have dominion over me.

Reader 2:   Deliver me from the oppression of man

Reader 1:   so will I keep your precepts.

Reader 2:   Make your face to shine upon me

Reader 1:   and teach me your statutes.

Reader 2:   Rivers of waters run down my eyes,

Reader 1:   because they keep not your law.

Reader 2:   Amen.

Faithfulness of God
Adapted Psalm 119:137-144
Readers 1,2

Introduction

Reader 1: The ways of the Lord are extolled,

Reader 2:   while the reading expresses the insignificance of man.

Reader 1: The writer seems tormented,

Reader 2:   yet he found solace in the righteousness of God.

Reader 1: Perhaps this may be your experience as well.

Reader 2: Listen as we read from Psalm 119:137-144.

Psalm 119:137-144

Reader 1: Righteous are you, O Lord,

Reader 2:   and upright are your judgments.

Reader 1: Your laws that you have commanded

Reader 2:   are righteous and very faithful.

Reader 1: My zeal has consumed me

Reader 2:   because my enemies have forgotten your words.

Reader 1: Your word is very pure.

Reader 2: I love it!

Reader 1: I am small and despised,

Reader 2:   yet I do not forget your precepts.

Reader 1: Your righteousness is an everlasting righteousness,

Reader 2:   and your law is the truth.

Reader 1: Trouble and anguish have taken hold on me,

Reader 2:   yet your commandments are my delights.

Reader 1: The righteousness of your laws is everlasting.

Reader 2: Give me understanding.

Reader 1: Give me understanding and I shall live.

The Lord Hears

Adapted from Psalm 119:145-152

Reader 1,2, Audience, Choir

Introduction

Reader 1:   The Psalmist cries unto the Lord

Reader 2:   to be heard and saved.

Reader 1:   He expresses hope and confidence

Reader 2:   in the commandments of God.

Reader 1:   Let's read together Psalm 119:145-152.

Psalm 119:145-152

Reader 1:   I cried with my whole being.

Audience: Hear me, O Lord,

Choir: Save me, O Lord,

Reader 2:   I will keep your statutes.

Reader 1:   I will keep your testimonies.

Reader 2:   Before the dawning of the morning I cried:

Audience: Hear me, O Lord,

Choir: Save me, O Lord,

Reader 1:   I have hope in your word.

Reader 2:   During the night watches my eyes were wide open

Reader 1:   that I might meditate in your word.

Reader 2:   Hear my voice according to your loving kindness.

Reader 1:   O Lord, quicken me according to your judgment.

Reader 2:   They come close who follow after evil.

Reader 1:   They are far from your law.

Audience: You come closer, O Lord!

Choir: All your commandments are true.

Reader 2:   Concerning your testimonies,

Reader 1:   I have known of old

Reader 2:   before the foundation of the world.

Reader 1:   Thanks be to God for these words.

Salvation
Adapted from Psalm 119:153-160
Readers 1,2

Introduction

Reader 1: The Psalmist, probably David, feels that the persecution
Reader 2:   from his enemies can only be avoided
Reader 1:   by the continual presence of God.
Reader 2: He affirms the enduring righteous judgments of God.
Reader 1: Listen for the reading taken from Psalm 119:153-160.

Psalm 119:153-160

Reader 1: Consider mine affliction
Reader 2:   and deliver me,
Reader 1:   because I have not forgotten your law.
Reader 2: Defend my cause,
Reader 1:   deliver me,
Reader 2:   make me alive according to your word.
Reader 1: Salvation is far from the wicked
Reader 2:   because they obey not your statutes.
Reader 1: Great are your tender mercies, O Lord,
Reader 2:   make me alive according to your judgments.
Reader 1: Many are my persecutors and my enemies,
Reader 2:   yet I have not turned from your testimonies.
Reader 1: I saw the sinners, and was grieved
Reader 2:   because they kept not your word.
Reader 1: Consider how I love your precepts.
Reader 2: Make me alive, O Lord,
Reader 1:   according to your loving kindness.
Reader 2: Your word is true from the beginning
Reader 1:   and every one of your righteous judgments.
Reader 2: Your righteous judgments endure forever.

Standing for Law and God
Adapted from Psalm 119:161-168
Readers 1,2, Choir

Introduction
Reader 1:   The Psalmist seems to be justifying his life before God.

Reader 2:   This text tells of his great love for God's law

Reader 1:   and how he has faithfully kept it.

Reader 2:   Listen as we read together in Psalm 119:161-168.

Psalm 119:161-168
Reader 1:   Princes have persecuted me without a cause,

Reader 2:   but my heart stands in awe of your word.

Choir: I rejoice at your word

Reader 2:   as one that finds great spoil.

Reader 1:   I hate and abhor lying,

Reader 2:   but your law do I love.

Choir: Seven times a day do I praise you

Reader 2:   because of your righteous judgments.

Choir: Great peace have they which love your law

Reader 2:   and nothing shall offend them.

Choir: Lord, I have hoped for your salvation

Reader 2:   and have done your commandments.

Reader 1:   My whole being has kept your testimonies

Reader 2:   and I love them exceedingly.

Reader 1:   I have kept your precepts and your laws

Reader 2:   for all my ways are before you.

Choir: This ends the reading.

Testimony to the Lord
Adapted from Psalm 119:169-176
Readers 1,2

Introduction

Reader 2: The author prays for understanding and deliverance

Reader 1:   as he longs for salvation.

Reader 2: He concludes by pleading with God

Reader 1:   to find and save his lost soul.

Reader 2: And now, Psalm 119:169-176.

Psalm 119:169-176

Reader 1: My voice pleads, O Lord,

Reader 2:   give me understanding according to your word.

Reader 1: My supplication is before you, O Lord,

Reader 2:   deliver me according to your word.

Reader 1: My lips shall ever praise you, O Lord,

Reader 2:   since you have taught me your statutes.

Reader 1: My tongue shall speak of your word, O Lord,

Reader 2:   for all your commandments are righteousness.

Reader 1: My body has chosen your precepts.

Reader 2: Let your hand help me!

Reader 1: My being longs for your salvation, O Lord,

Reader 2:   your law is my delight.

Reader 1: As long as my being lives;

Reader 2:   it shall praise you

Reader 1:   and let your judgments help me.

Reader 2: I have gone astray like a lost sheep.

Reader 1: O Lord, find your lost servant

Reader 2:   for I do not forget your commandments.

Reader 1: Amen.

The Lord Is My Help
Taken from Psalm 120 & 121
Reader 1,2, Audience, Choir

Introduction

Reader 1: The Psalmist longs for salvation
Reader 2:   from the evils that surround him.
Reader 1: He concludes that salvation comes only from the Lord,
Reader 2:   who does not rest until preservation is assured.
Reader 1: Let us read together from Psalm 120 and 121.

Psalm 120 and 121

Reader 1: In my distress I cried unto the Lord
Audience: and He heard me.
Reader 2: Now save me, O Lord,
Audience: from lying lips
Choir: and from deceitful tongues.
Reader 1: What shall be done to those false tongues?
Audience: Punish them with sharp arrows,
Choir: burn them with coals of juniper tree!
Reader 1: Woe is me in my travels
Reader 2:   as I dwell in tents!
Reader 1: My being has long lived
Reader 2:   with those who hate peace.
Audience: I am for peace,
Reader 1:   but when I speak,
Reader 2:   they are for war.
Reader 1: So,
Reader 2:   I will lift up mine eyes unto the hills,
Reader 1:   but where does my help come from?
Audience: My help comes from the LORD
Choir: who made heaven and earth.
Reader 1: He will not allow my foot to be moved.

Audience: The Lord that keeps me does not sleep!

Reader 2:   Behold, He that keeps Israel

Reader 1:   shall neither slumber nor sleep.

Audience: The Lord is my keeper.

Choir: The Lord is my shade

Reader 1:   from the sun that can burn me at midday

Reader 2:   nor from the moon by night.

Reader 1:   The LORD shall keep me from all evil.

Audience: He shall preserve my soul.

Reader 2:   The LORD shall preserve my going out

Audience: and my coming in

Reader 1:   from this time forth,

Choir: and even for evermore.

Reader 2:   This ends the reading.

I Look to the Lord
Adapted from Psalm 123 & 124
Readers 1,2, Audience, Choir

Introduction

Reader 1: The writer compares God's care

Reader 2:   to how a faithful master treats his servants.

Reader 1: Notice the repetition of the words:

Reader 2:   if it had not been the Lord

Reader 1:   who was on our side.

Reader 2: Let us read together from Psalm 123 & 124.

Psalm 123 & 124

Reader 1: I lift up mine eyes to you, O Lord,

Reader 2:   who dwells in the heavens.

Reader 1: As the eyes of servants look

Reader 2:   to the hand of their masters,

Reader 1:   as the eyes of a maid looks

Reader 2:   to the hand of her mistress

Reader 1:   so our eyes look

Reader 2:   to the Lord our God

Reader 1:   until He will have mercy on us.

Audience: O Lord, do have mercy upon us

Reader 2:   for we are surrounded with contempt.

Reader 1: The arrogant and proud

Reader 2:   completely fill us with scorn and ridicule.

Choir: However, if it had not been the Lord

Audience: who was on our side,

Reader 1:   when men rose up against us:

Reader 2:   they would have quickly swallowed us up.

Choir: If it had not been the Lord

Audience: who was on our side,

Reader 1:   when their wrath was kindled against us

153

Reader 2:   the waters would have overwhelmed us,
Reader 1:   the proud waters had gone over our being.
Choir: If it had not been the LORD
Audience: who was on our side
Reader 2:   we would have been devoured by their teeth.
Reader 1:   We would have been trapped
Reader 2:   as a bird in the snare of the fowlers,
Reader 1:   but the snare is broken
Reader 2:   and we are escaped.
Choir: It was the LORD
Audience: who was on our side.
Reader 2:   Our help is in the name of the LORD
Reader 1:   who made heaven and earth.
Audience: Blessed be the name of the Lord.

A Psalm of David

Adapted from Psalm 139

Readers 1,2,3,4, Audience

Introduction

Reader 1: This reading is a personal prayer of David,

Reader 2:   as he comes face to face

Reader 1:   with the majesty, the bigness,

Reader 2:   with the omnipresence, the all knowingness,

Reader 1:   and with the power of God.

Reader 2: Psalm 139 is perhaps the grandest of the Psalms.

Reader 1: It exalts the power of God!

Reader 2: Let the audience join with us

Reader 1:   as we read the "Crown of Psalms".

Psalm 139

Reader 1: Oh Lord, you know me so well:

Reader 3:   wherever I sit,

Reader 2:   wherever I stand,

Reader 4:   wherever I lie down,

Reader 2:   whatever I think,

Reader 3:   whatever I say,

Audience: I know it all completely.

Reader 1: Your hand is on me.

Audience: I am before and behind you.

Reader 2: Your knowledge overwhelms me.

Reader 4: How, tell me . . .

Reader 3:   tell me how, O Lord,

Reader 2:   where can I flee from your presence?

Reader 1: In the heavens?

Audience: No, I am there.

Reader 2: To the depths of the sea?

Audience: No, I am there as well!

Reader 3:   In the early morning?

Audience: No, I will be there!

Reader 4:   Then where can I hide from you, God?

Reader 3:   In the far side of the sea?

Reader 2:   Surely in the darkness,

Reader 1:   I can disappear from you?

Audience: No!

Reader 1:   God's hand will still guide me

Reader 4:   and His eyes will penetrate my inky darkness?

Reader 3:   Lord, we praise you because

Reader 2:   you created my inmost parts and formed me

Reader 1:   while I was still in my mother's womb.

Audience: I know you full well.

Reader 1:   You wove me together in the depths of the earth.

Audience: Your name is written in my book.

Reader 2:   If I count your praises day and night

Reader 3:   the number would be vast,

Reader 4:   outnumbering the sands of the sea.

Reader 1:   When I awake . . .

Audience: I am still with you.

Reader 3:   How precious are your thoughts to me, O Lord.

Reader 1:   Search me, God.

Audience: I know your heart.

Reader 1:   Test me.

Audience: I know your anxious thoughts.

Reader 3:   Tell me if I have any offensive way

Reader 2:   and lead me in the way everlasting.

Reader 1:   Oh Lord, you know me so well!

Reader 4:   Amen.

Celebrate God-A Call to Worship

Adapted from Psalms 147-150

Readers 1,2, Audience

Introduction

Reader 1: The reading today is wonderful way
to introduce our worship service.

Reader 2: It recounts the creation of the world.

Reader 1: It talks about God's love.

Reader 2: It is an invitation to worship and celebrate our God.

Reader 1: Let us read together Psalm 147 to 150.

Psalm 147 to 150

Reader 1: How good it is to celebrate God's presence.

Reader 2: How good it is to sing His praises throughout each day.

Audience: Let's celebrate what He has done!

Reader 2: He has done so much for us:

Reader 1:   created the world,

Reader 2:   made the sun and moon,

Reader 1:   lighted unnumbered stars in the universe,

Reader 2:   put creatures that swim and crawl

Reader 1:   and walk and fly on our earth.

Audience: We have enjoyed these gifts.

Reader 1: Praise Him for His devoted servants:

Reader 2:   who communicated His word,

Reader 1:   who performed His miracles,

Reader 2:   who brought His healing to people's hurts.

Audience: They have blessed our lives.

Reader 2: God continues to bless our world with

Reader 1:   flowers that bloom in glorious color,

Reader 2:   rains that freshen the earth,

Reader 1:   and birds that fill the air with song.

Audience: Thanks be to God for his perpetual love.
Reader 1: He does love us!
Reader 2: He pursues those of us who run from Him.
Reader 1: He reaches out to heal us and to draw us to Himself.
Reader 2: He has forgiven us. Praise God!
Audience: He is worthy of your praise.
Reader 2: We will proclaim His love.
Reader 1: Singing His glories to all.
Reader 2: Those of you who write or paint,
Audience: write and paint of the Lord.
Reader 2: Those of you who dance and play,
Audience: dance and play of the Lord.
Reader 2: Those of you who preach and teach,
Audience: preach and teach of the Lord.
Reader 2: Those of you who make music,
Audience: make music of the Lord.
Reader 2: Those of you who are alive,
Audience: live and give of the Lord.
Reader 2: Let's celebrate!
Reader 1: Celebrate with music and poetry and art
Reader 2: with movement and friendship and gifts.
Reader 1: Let us all join in celebrating the majesty
of our great and loving God.
Reader 2: Let the music begin.
Reader 1: Let the processional begin.
Audience: Thanks be to God.
Reader 2: Let the celebration begin!
Reader 1: Let's worship God!